(RE)MAKING TRAGEDY

CHARLES MEE
and
GREEK DRAMA

KARELISA V. HARTIGAN

Table of Contents

Preface

Charles Mee's plays have been haunting the back of my mind for years.

His *Orestes 2.0* first came to my attention when I was writing my book *Greek Tragedy on the American Stage.* The reviews of his first Greek-based play immediately caught my attention as did the included pictures of the En Garde Arts production on the abandoned pier on the Hudson River. Some years later the Drama Department at the University of Florida produced *Big Love*; I was struck by the bright beauty of the performance but at the time did not see exactly how it could be connected to Aeschylus' early tragedy. I left it in my memory and went on to other things.

Throughout my professional academic career I have read, studied, and taught Greek tragedy, and seen as many productions as possible. A major goal in my pursuit of the Greek classics has been to point out how the ancient world is relevant to the modern, how the Greek myths are retold today, and what impact they make upon a time so distant and different from their inception. My interest has especially focused on the retelling of the ancient myths in post-classical drama. Charles Mee's (re)made Greek plays exactly match my interest and intent.

When early in 2010 I was invited to write a chapter for a collection of essays on contemporary dramatic revisions of myth and legend, Mee's plays immediately came to mind. Although for that essay I considered only my old favorite, *Orestes 2.0* (there linking my discussion of this play with A.R. Gurney's *Another Antigone*), I realized I wanted to read all of his Greek based plays. Because Mee so conveniently – and generously – posts his plays on the web, I was able to access and read them easily.

In reading the seven plays (re)made from Greek tragedies, I had various reactions. I found them in many ways bizarre: what were all these catalogues of the flotsam and jetsam of modern life doing in the ancient stories? I was also at times repulsed: what did all these graphic descriptions and sexually explicit lines have to do with anything from the Greek world? Mostly I was intrigued: the familiar tragedies of Aeschylus and Euripides were still there behind the modern distractions: how did Mee do that? And, finally, he called them tragedies. If Mee's plays are tragedies, I thought I must seek a new definition of tragedy, one applicable for today. Thus my quest began.

In this book I discuss the ancient plays from which Mee drew his inspiration and his (re)making of those plays. From my analysis of what he has done with the old tales, I posit a new definition of tragedy. Aristotle's classic description still holds true, for these news dramas do arouse emotions of pity and fear. But in the modern world there are different forces at work, different influences on the lives of men and women. Charles Mee's plays address those forces and influences in a way that is both uniquely his own and widely applicable.

Although there are some (but not many) books and articles about Charles Mee's work, in writing this book I have relied extensively on reviews of Mee's plays. At this moment in time, his works seem to be of more interest to those who do theater than those who discuss it. But in talking about his plays with various people I kept hearing that they rather liked the performance but really had no idea exactly what the show was about, how were they related to the ancient myths, why he called his work (re)made Greek stories. I wrote this book to be a guide to the audiences who will see Mee's plays, to help them understand what he is doing, why he is doing it, and how wonderfully he has (re)made the ancient stories into something new and significant.

As I finished the initial drafts of the book, I had the opportunity to meet with Charles Mee and discuss his plays. As a classicist I do not have the opportunity to meet with those who wrote the plays I read. So here I wish to acknowledge what a pleasure it was to meet this talented, charming, and delightful playwright. It has been a pleasure to write about his work.

Acknowledgements

Charles Mee himself stands first among those to whom I owe appreciation. I want to thank Verna Foster, whose invitation to contribute a chapter to her book on modern versions of ancient myths turned my attention back to Mee's plays. I owe my greatest gratitude to my husband, Kevin McCarthy, who helped me put this manuscript in the form necessary for submission, and for his continued support and encouragement, making sure I wrote 500 (or more) words every day.

Introduction

In this study I discuss the Greek plays of Charles Mee's "(re)making" project: the three plays of his *Imperial Dreams* trilogy: *Orestes 2.0, Agamemnon 2.0, and Iphigeneia 2.0,* the three he titles "Tragedies," *Bacchae 2.1, Trojan Women – A Love Story,* and *True Love,* and the "Comedy" *Big Love.* My quest is to show how Mee has adapted the ancient plays, which everyone would agree fit most standard definitions of a tragedy, into something so different that it may be necessary to redefine "tragedy" for the modern stage.

The plays written by the three tragic playwrights of ancient Athens, Aeschylus, Sophocles, and Euripides, have often been chosen for production in the commercial theaters of America. Especially since the decade of the 1960s, producers and directors have offered a goodly selection of the thirty-three extant tragedies and the eleven comedies of Aristophanes on their stages. But even more popular for modern productions are the plays based on the ancient scripts; up-dated versions or entirely new creations may be seen in theaters in the Americas and Europe. There are, for example, a veritable plethora of recent plays based on the story of Antigone. This is not surprising, as the number of harsh rulers is ever increasing and there is widespread admiration for the individual who stands up against a misguided misuse of power, usually in the political arena but in corporations and academia as well. And while college and university administrators may think that the language, literature, and culture of ancient Greece are passé and not worthy of support, students and the general public alike find the ancient stories important and compelling. Thus playwrights who choose to pen scripts based on the ancient myths or new versions of the ancient plays can have every confidence that their work will find an audience.

1

The idea of rewriting existing plays dates from the Greeks themselves and was certainly followed by the Romans. Euripides retold the stories of Aeschylus and Sophocles, while Seneca turned to Euripides' texts for his tragedies and for his comedies Plautus turned to those of Menander and other comic poets of ancient Athens (whose works exist for us mostly in fragments). Shakespeare mined the Roman scripts and almost every playwright since has turned to the classic myths for inspiration. In the twentieth century the French writers, Anouilh, Cocteau, Gide, Giraudoux, and Sartre, for example, all wrote plays based on extant Greek dramas, while in America such writers as Robinson Jeffers, William Faulkner, Eugene O'Neill, most especially in *Mourning Becomes Electra*, his trilogy based on the House of Atreus myth, and more recently, Lee Brewer with Robert Telson, John Barton, and Sarah Ruhl.

Thus when Charles Mee began his "(re)making" project he was in good company. He admits right up front that he has "pillaged" the ancient texts for his own work, asserting that "there is no such thing as an original play." Certain of this fact, he has often taken the ancient texts verbatim, allowing characters from the Athenian stage to say the words of Euripides in a similar context – but in entirely new settings. His dramas might well be (and often are) described as a collage of past and present, juxtaposed and jammed against each other. Pieces of the contemporary world, taken from every medium that daily assaults the eyes and mind of men and women today, are culled by Mee for his new creations. He claims that he uses the classic text as "scaffolding" on which to hang his own construction; he then smashes the new piece into fragments and presents it held together in a different way.(1) In (re) making his plays drawn from the Greek, he sometimes offers an almost direct translation or transposition interspersed with several passages of contemporary comments, at other times he changes the theme as well as the form and the ancient text is only there as a vague haunting presence the audience seeks to recall.(2) Thus we see Mee's Agamemnon give the lines of Euripides' character from the *Iphigenia at Aulis* in Mee's *Iphigenia 2.0*, or his Orestes speak the words of the Greek Orestes, but the crazed son of Agamemnon is now in a mental hospital, not at the palace of Mycenae.

Mee wrote the plays I discuss here in the fifteen years from 1992 to 2007. These were years in which America was involved in wars overseas, wars about which many people had doubts and against which many people protested. Mee has always been an ardent pacifist and takes every opportunity to rail against the inhumanity of war and the suffering it creates. Thus in the war-based dramas of ancient Greece he found a readily accessible source to "pillage." The Athenian dramatists were military men and wrote for an audience of men who had experienced war first hand. The ancient Greek male was eligible for military service from age 18 to age 60, so the chances of any man making it to the end of his life without picking up a weapon in war were slim. Indeed, the low average life-span for an ancient Greek is based upon war deaths more than life-style; those who survived battle could expect to have long lives – the playwrights themselves lived into their 80s and 90s.

While the major themes of Greek tragedies rest upon familial conflicts – disputes, religious controversy, misguided passions, betrayals – many deal directly with the results of war, while others, written during times of military conflicts, show the results of these conflicts on those who fight in or return from them. There can be little doubt but that Euripides used the stage of Dionysus' theater to speak out against war in his *Trojan Women, Helen,* and *Iphigeneia at Aulis.* In his *Heracles* he shows the hero returning from the exhausting completion of his god-assigned labors, choosing to present the hero as broken in mind if not in body, a man unable to fit back into his family life. In his play Heracles suffers from such delusions, compulsion to violence, and a desire for suicide as do soldiers returning from the wars in Iraq and Afghanistan in the early years of the twenty-first century.

But Sophocles, too, a man who knew war first-hand, wrote plays showing the devastating effects of war. His earliest extant play, *Ajax,* shows a man driven mad when his commanders and fellow officers do not properly recognize his battle valor, a man then driven to suicide in his shame. These same early twentieth century wars record not only many soldiers' desire for death but also that more soldiers commit suicides than in any previous military conflict. Sophocles' penultimate extant play, *Philoctetes*, shows how an army will isolate a man who is physically unfit for battle, how society also isolates the man suffering from severe wounds.

Mee has read the plays of Euripides and taken them as the basis for his anti-war message. He might have found appropriate themes in Sophocles' dramas, but Euripides, considered to be the most iconoclastic of the ancient dramatic trio, is generally considered by readers today as the most "modern," the one who speaks most appropriately for the current stage. This judgment is, of course, not limited to the contemporary critic: Aristophanes in several of his comedies, especially in the *Frogs*, condemned his tragedy-writing colleague for his too-modern viewpoints. In that play the god of drama crosses to Hades to restore a dramatist who can restore ancient values to Athens. Although Dionysus started out to bring back the youngest dramatist, upon testing the playwrights he determined that Euripides was not the proper one for the job and chose Aeschylus as the dramatist who held the appropriate values and viewpoints to restore Athens to her former glory. But time has finally awarded Euripides pride of place: what lost him restoration in Aristophanes' judgment brings him victory in the contemporary world, for it is his plays that are most frequently staged and, with two exceptions, his are the texts that Charles Mee chose to plunder in his (re)making project.

Charles Mee's use of music before and during his plays also needs comment. The chorus of the ancient dramas sang (and danced) to music; the lyric monologues were voiced to musical accompaniment. Each of Mee's plays also has a choral group appropriate for the theme and whose presence is as natural as is that of the ancient choruses of citizens or attendants. These perform contemporary songs drawn from a multiplicity of sources; main characters also sing from time to time, Mee's equivalent of the lyric passages of their Greek counterparts. The contemporary songs Mee chooses might, when first heard, seem to be part of the "extras" tacked onto his plays. But the various musical pieces and popular songs are well tied to the story line of each play. We might expect – and get –

wedding marches in *Big Love*. Modern Greek folk songs open *Iphigeneia 2.0*, and variations play throughout the drama, from Brian Nubian's *A Soldier's Story* to underscore the words of the Soldier Chorus to Hadjidakis' *Never on Sunday* in the scene between Clytemnestra and Achilles: the first is directly appropriate, the second adds a light touch to the scene which is humorous in Euripides' original play as well. But other musical additions are more subtle. In the second half of his *Trojan Women,* based on Vergil's *Aenei*d IV, Mee's chorus of women sing the Cowboy Junkies' version of *Blue Moon*, appropriate for the Dido and Aeneas story Mee tells here. In *True Love*, Mee's take on the Hippolytus story, a take far removed from the original, various members of the cast form a garage band, while a radio either blasts out the strident noise of Screamin' Jay Hawkins' performance of *I Put a Spell on You*, or, at the close of the action, plays Hank Snow's (surprisingly sunny) rendition of *I Don't Hurt Anymore*, floating out over a stage filled with dead bodies. Mee often gives options for the music, but whatever song a director chooses must be appropriate for his theme.

Another characteristic of Mee's scripts also demands notice. He fills his pages with numerous stage directions, character descriptions, and suggestions for the director and cast to take into account as they mount a performance. He does not give a specific piece of music but offers a number of possible options. He breaks into the script to suggest how the action is to be understood. He paints a verbal picture of how a scene is to be performed, giving far more complex directions than the usual blocking suggestion found in most playbooks. Mee's most unusual inset into a play occurs when he gives two totally different options for the action, writing in that a character is to be killed — or not. In *Trojan Women - A Love Story*, for example, Mee's stage directions read:

> While the chorus sings this final song,
> Aeneas drags himself from the hot tub.
> He is nearly dead—
> or else, he doesn't drag himself from the tub,
> and he is dead.

And he claims he does not care which option a cast chooses; he requests only that the decision be true to their understanding of the play.

While five of Mee's Greek-based tragedies take texts from Euripides, his *Agamemnon 2.0* rests on the drama of the same name by Aeschylus; the Greek *Agamemnon* stands as Act I of the *Oresteia* trilogy. Mee's modern play is rather closely modeled on that of Aeschylus and is a play that shows the King-Commander caught in the glory of his conquest and how his hybris is punished by his wife, not the gods. Aeschylus had boldly shown how revenge could be linked to sex and violence and Mee has directly followed his lead in his own *Agamemnon*.

It is also to Aeschylus that Mee turned for the Greek play he terms a comedy, *Big Love*. Although based on the tragic *Suppliant Maidens*, Mee takes the odd legend of wedding night murders and (re)makes it into a comedy about love and marriage. He sets the action in a seaside villa in Italy and casts the suitors as fast-talking Greek-American men who arrive by helicopter. Wild physical action marks the play, which with Mee's typical eclectic dialogue makes *Big Love* more comic than tragic. In the end, of course, only one couple, Nikos and Lydia, survives, and Mee's stage directions indicate that theirs may not be a happy marriage. As the plays he terms "tragedies" have aspects that are in many ways comic, so the ending of his "comedy" *Big Love* is ambiguous. Perhaps Mee's listing of the play as a comedy is the reason that this Greek-based play is the one most often performed – far more frequently than is the Aeschylean original.

In the other five plays in this series Mee starts from those of Euripides. His *Orestes 2.0* is particularly close to its Greek original, as is *Iphigeneia 2.0* to Euripides' last play, *Iphigeneia at Aulis*. Mee's *Bacchae 2.1* follows the story line of Euripides' play of the same name, but he introduces far more sex than the Greek playwright even suggests. *Trojan Women - a Love Story* moves from Euripides' condemnation of war in his 415 BC tragedy to a very free retelling of Book IV of Vergil's *Aeneid*. Finally, in *True Love*, supposedly based on Euripides' *Hippolytus*, Mee has smashed the ancient framework so violently that only an audience member well-versed in both Euripidean and Mee-an dramas can recognize the original frame.

But in Mee's Greek (re)making project, there remains, with the possible exception of *True Love*, a visible connection between his work and the ancient texts from which he started his plays. The myths remain virtually unchanged, the lines are often repeated verbatim from old text to new and the ideas presented on the Athenian stage are expressed in Mee's various dramatic spaces. He, like Euripides, in particular, but also in the manner of Aeschylus and Sophocles, speaks out against the violence and madness of war, the ruin resulting from lust misplaced, the suffering men and women cause to each other, often deliberately but more frequently by random chance.

Charles Mee's plays are entirely new creations: he has (re)made the ancient plays into scripts for the modern stage, showing his audience a world that is at times strange and, at other times, frighteningly familiar. The strange and the familiar aspects which we recognize in Mee's plays come from the world in which we live. This is not an unexpected result, for the playwright intends his audience to come to that recognition by including in his scripts all that he sees around us. He once described his writing method thus:

> I love to make plays that feel like my life in this way —
> and that don't hide what is appropriated or sampled or stolen
> from others. So when I look at my own plays onstage, I can see
> what came from the inside of my head and what came from the
> world, from MTV and Soap Opera Digest and the op-ed page of
> The Times. Stories and songs and dances, pieces of found text,
> overheard conversations, classical plays, dances from Bollywood,
> opinions that come straight off a television talk show, stuff from
> the Internet. My plays feel like my life — a life lived inside my
> head and in the world at the same time. I call the way these plays
> are made "realism."(3)

In this all-inclusive world each man and woman must find a way to create — or (re)create — a meaning that responds to a world of which they have but a small part in defining. The modern world is shaped more by its prevalent culture than by deities such as those in whom the ancients believed. According to Charles Mee's dramas, we are on our own.

CHAPTER 1
Charles L. Mee

During the course of his writing career, Charles Mee has used various forms of his name. Depending on context, he calls himself Charles L. Mee, Jr., Charles L. Mee, Charles Mee; he is Chuck Mee to his friends. The practice reflects Mee's own understanding of literature and exemplifies how he writes: texts are out there in the public sphere along with all other aspects of society, and there is no form that is so fixed it cannot be changed.

Charles L. Mee, Jr. was born on September 15, 1938 and raised in Barrington, Illinois. His early childhood years were happy, filled with family events and a love of – and ability in – sports. His dream was to play quarterback for Notre Dame.

But when he was fourteen, during a family trip in the summer of 1953, polio attacked him violently, forcing him to spend many months isolated in the local hospital. Mee documents his illness and his fight through it in *A Nearly Normal Life.*(4) Mee learned to adjust his walking to the braces; he learned that only he could overcome the tendency to anger or despair that threatened him as he realized he would not ever live the life he had envisioned. In his autobiography he shows how he adjusted his physical and psychological perspectives to his new reality. Suffice to say that he was successful in his efforts and finished up his high school courses on time while participating in as many activities as possible.

He reports that even after he had been cured, he realized that he had to undergo recovery again and again. He had to re-invent his physical life at every step of his existence, and his psychological life at every turn of events. He also tells how the experience influenced his writing style. His life had been shattered like a crystal goblet and even the collected pieces cannot be remade into a whole glass. Thus he prefers to write sentence fragments rather than flowing paragraphs, and leave intact people to write intact books:

> To me, sentences should veer and smash up, careen out of control…break off and come to a sighing inconclusiveness. . . My body of work, to feel true to me must feel fragmented. And then, too, if you find it hard to walk down the sidewalk, you like, in the freedom of your mind, to make a sentence that leaps and dances now and then before it comes to a sudden stop.(5)

During his time in hospital, isolated, and suffering extreme pain and fear, Mee realized, he later wrote, that he had the strength and the will to try and survive the disease that wracked him. His case was so dire that his father called in a priest to administer last rites. At that moment, Mee writes, he "became an ex-Catholic;" the church had not prayed for him to live but had written him off to death.(6) This was a second step into the new way he would forever view the world: a man can survive and can do it without the aid of the organized church. The high school football coach inadvertently taught him a third lesson: people would lie to him, tell him what they wanted him to hear, what they wanted to believe. At an early age, Mee learned to rely on himself, to endure isolation, and that it was up to him to overcome alienation and to be responsible for his thoughts and beliefs.

During his convalescence, one gift made a profound and positive change on his life. His high school English teacher, Maude Strouss, gave him a copy of Plato's *Symposium*. Mee realized he would have to rely on his mind, not his body from that moment on, so he read the book, and then asked for more Plato. As he reflected upon his teacher's gift of Plato's book on love, he realized she had given him not only a book but a gift of love; he writes: "Her gift has informed my entire life."(7) From Plato his reading extended to history, so that by the time he was able to return to school, he had completed on his own a veritable course in western civilization.

As he returned to live outside the hospital, Mee realized daily the changes the disease had made in his life. First he had to deal with the physical challenges that daily assaulted his body, and then he had to deal with the psychological issues that a crippled body imposed. As cited above, Mee noted how the physical limitations of his body influenced his writing style. I suggest that maybe it also influenced the style he developed for the on-stage action in several of his plays. In both *Big Love* and *True Love*, for example, whole scenes are devoted to wild and untamed physical displays. In his stage directions for *Big Love*, he states that "the over-the-top extremity of this physical work should establish the kind of physical piece this is." Characters throw themselves over and over to the ground in what becomes a rhythmic sequence of violent action. The final scenes of his plays are often chaotic displays of unrestrained movement. Through his drama personae, perhaps, Mee can engage in the contact sports he had hoped to play until disease blocked his dream.

Mee also read extensively; he was guided in his reading by an advisor, Alan Peshkin, with whom Mee went into Chicago to visit secondhand bookstores. Through his own interests and Peshkin's guidance Mee selected books that would not be expected to be on the reading list of a young man his age, and many that both his father and the Church thought he should not read; his enjoyment of Machiavelli's *The Prince*, for example, caused his father to be especially angry.(8) Perhaps because of his extensive reading, Mee soon became a writer. He could not play sports but he could write about them, and began to compose a column for his school's weekly newspaper. As he broadened his topics, he pondered the idea that he would become a writer. When his friends asked him what he had to say, he pondered that, too:

> I had nothing to say; it was just something I could do sitting down. It wasn't until years later that I realized that writing is not saying something, it is about discovering something.(9)

And so Charles Mee went off to college, where he first majored in history, then turned to literature, art history, and theater. After graduating from Harvard in 1960, he settled in the Greenwich Village area of New York, and embarked upon a writing (and editing) career. He became involved in the local theater scene of Off and Off-Off Broadway, writing his first plays there and directing others. To cover his expenses he took an editing job at American Heritage publishing company. He first started as a fact checker, and then eventually he became the editor of the hardback bi-monthly *Horizon: A Magazine of the Arts*. While this was a magazine for the general (and well-educated) public, Mee also served as the Advising Editor and then Contributing Editor of *TDR* (*Tulane Drama Review* / now: *Drama Review*) until 1964 and its Associate Editor from 1964 to 1965.

During this time he also became involved in anti-war politics and became co-founder and chair of the National Committee on the Presidency, "dedicated to the impeachment of the man he referred to as 'the Dark Liar.'" (10) His distrust of and disgust with the Vietnam War brought him back to the study of history and especially of previous wars. He turned his pen to writing anti-war treatises and books about past military conflicts, hoping to arouse the public conscience about the destruction and suffering these caused. His *Meeting at Potsdam* (1975) is a close study of the three leaders, Truman, Churchill, and Stalin when they met at the small German town of Potsdam in 1945. He gained access to the letters of those who participated in the conference as well as using other historical documents. Mee described this key event in history in a manner that reflects his playwriting skill; the book was so readable that it was chosen as a main selection of the Literary Guild, and was adapted as a film for television by David Susskind. The success of *Meeting at*

Potsdam allowed Mee to live well off its royalties for some time. He wrote several more historical books during the next decade before returning to playwriting.(11) He turned back to history one last time in 1993 to write his final historical work, *Playing God: Seven Fateful Moments When Great Men Met to Change the World*, a book which discusses several significant political meetings among leaders as diverse as Pope Leo the Great and Attila the Hun (who met in Italy in 452) to the political leaders who met at the G-7 summit in London in 1991. As with his book on Potsdam and other books of history, Mee's sense of theater made his non-fiction works accessible to the general reader.

When asked in a recent interview why he had switched from writing history to writing plays, Mee responded:

> One of the reasons I stopped writing history was that I felt trapped in a form of discourse that seemed false to me. The form of history, I thought, required me to frame rational, dispassionate statements about the world that were meant to contain the truth, but they were statements about a world that made you want to weep and shriek and cry out. And that content wasn't allowed. Somehow, the theater allows me to use both my mind and my heart.(12)

As theater influenced his history books, so history influenced his dramas. From the very beginning of his playwriting career, Mee has penned plays that address political and social issues. His topics and his public persona led him to be described as "The accidental historian [who] had become a citizen playwright."(13) His first play to attract wide attention was *The Investigation of the Murder in El Salvador*, which was staged in 1984 at the Mark Taper in Los Angeles under the direction of Gordon Davidson. Two years later (1986) Mee persuaded the directors of the Vienna Project, Martha Clarke and Lyn Austin to let him write the text for their visual image production. Mee and Clarke's *Vienna: Lusthaus* won the Obie for best play that year and audiences crowded in to see its run at Joseph Papp's Public Theater.

Over the years Mee has tended to write plays united in theme, even if none of them forms a distinct or deliberate trilogy or tetralogy. His first series of plays offered political topics, clearly a reflection of his interest in theater and devotion to anti-war literature. The Pan-American tetralogy is comprised of *The Investigation of the Murder in El Salvador* (in which no investigation takes place), *The Constitutional Convention: A Sequel* (in which no figures from America's constitutional convention appear), *The War to End War* (with an act taking place at the moment of signing of the Treaty of Versailles in 1919 and another at Los Alamos), with *The Imperialists at the Club Cave Canem* (a performance piece without a specific meaning) rounding out the series.(14) In later years he would write a "trilogy" on love, while three of the Greek-based plays I discuss here form a thematic trilogy. There are, of course, many other separate pieces in his extensive catalogue of plays.

Mee's life beyond the theater was still connected with it. He married several times and several of his wives were actresses. While still at Harvard and directing Brecht's *The Good Woman of Setzuan*, he fell in love with and married Claire Lu Thomas, the leading woman; it was a short marriage. In 1962 Mee married Suzi Baker, with whom he had his daughter Erin and his son Charles L. Mee III; but this marriage lasted only until 1975. His third wife was the actress and playwright Kathleen Tolan, who played the lead in the initial staging of *The Imperialists at the Club Cave Canem*. Mee's daughter Erin, who would also continue a career in theater, directing, acting, and currently (2010) is teaching drama at Swarthmore College, directed the Off-Off Broadway production. Sarah and Alice were born to Mee and Tolan in a marriage which also did not last. Finally Mee met and fell deeply in love with Laurie Williams, who was the inspiration for the "Love Trilogy" and played the lead in *True Love*. But this relationship, too, failed in 2001. Indeed, at the production of *True Love*, Mee was in the odd position (some might have said difficult) of seeing his ex-wife playing the lead in a play directed by his daughter. Mee married again several years ago; he and Michi adopted a daughter from China.

When Mee turned to writing dramas full time, he found a new style that shared little with his earlier prose, other than a passion for politics and a deep-rooted dislike of war. Once he entered upon playwriting, he developed a unique style. He once described his method as more closely related to what a painter does before his easel than a writer at his desk:

> I don't think I write plays the way playwrights write plays. I think I write plays the way painters paint paintings. Van Gogh did sunflowers: he didn't do one painting of a sunflower; he did many paintings of sunflowers, of fields of sunflowers, over and over again—more and more fields, this kind of field and that kind of field, in this kind of light and that kind of light. Painters do this all the time: they use the same subject matter; they reuse the same images in one painting after another. And I do that.(15)

More importantly, Mee created a collage style based on radical reconstructions of found texts. He considers his plays as "(re)making" of existing texts, ancient and modern; the (re) making is often radical, at other times far more subtle. After a number of historical plays (the Pan-American series), Mee turned to Greek mythology for his inspiration. And although the history plays —and others— kept coming from his computer, he became more widely known for those plays that begin with Greek tragedies.

Playwriting became a full-time occupation in the early 1990s and he turns out several scripts a year. Charles Mee has the luxury of devoting most of his day to writing because he, unique among playwrights, has a sponsor. In 1998 his long time friend, Richard Fisher, former chairman of Morgan Stanley, agreed to the half-joking proposition he made, that Fisher become his patron. Mee says his relationship with Fisher is far beyond that of the Medici's with Michelangelo, for Fisher has never asked Mee to write anything on his demand.(16) After Richard's death in 2004 his wife Jeanne has continued to be Mee's patron. In recent years Mee began teaching a graduate seminar on playwriting at Columbia University's Theater Department.

Although his first works were usually first produced by experimental and fringe theater groups, in recent years audiences can more frequently see his plays, especially those based on Greek originals, at more mainstream theaters in all major cities across the nation. He has garnered many awards for his work, which is also often performed in theaters abroad, especially Holland and Germany.(17) It can now be said that while his is not yet household name, people who know theater know Charles Mee's plays.

CHAPTER II

Part I

Ancient Athenian Drama

In the early spring of each year, the Athenians gathered together on the south slope of their Acropolis to celebrate the earth's rebirth by honoring Dionysus, the god associated with its annual regeneration. According to tradition, it was at his festival that Greek drama, both tragedy and comedy, began. While rituals and sacrifices marked all Greek festivals, several included pageants, and in the course of time those enacted for Dionysus developed into what we now know as Athenian drama. By the fifth century BC the event in Athens was known as the City Dionysia, a five-day festival for the god. The first day was devoted to sacrifices to Dionysus. During days two, three, and four, three tragedies and a satyr play, each day's presentation written by one playwright, were offered in the morning; in later years a comedy was presented in the evening of each day.

The fifth day of the festival was for the awarding of prizes. For although the City Dionysia was a festival in honor of a god, like most things in Greek life, the festival was also a competition: a prize was awarded to the playwright whom the official board of judges determined to have written the best play that year. At some point during the previous year the dramatists had submitted their plays, or the outlines of their plays, to the panel of judges. If they liked the script, they reported to the playwright that he had been "granted a chorus." This was the go-ahead for him to complete his scripts, select his cast, train the chorus: do all the things necessary to stage his plays. Plays, because each tragedian had to present three tragedies and a satyr play; the comedians only had to offer a single script. The winning playwright received a display tripod (as well as, most likely, a cash award).(18)

The plays were presented in a designated site on the south slope of the Athenian Acropolis, a defined acting and viewing space. The basic shape of the Greek theater was a sacred circle around which the audience sat. Some have said the first such space was the threshing floor, which in Greece is a circle of stone on a leveled space of a terraced hillside. Others have said the very idea of a circle is sacred and thus appropriate for the hymns and sacrifices for the god. Whatever its origin, the standard ancient theater consisted of the round *orchestra*, or dancing floor, with a low rectangular stage adjacent to it. As the Greek word for stage is the same as for tent, *skene*, giving our word scene, it has been suggested that the original stage building was merely a tent into which the actor could exit from the orchestra.

In Greek, drama means things done, theater comes from Greek words for seeing, so drama means things done before a watching audience. In the earliest days people gathered together and sat on the slope of the adjacent hillside, later on wooden seats and, by the mid-fifth century, the audience watched from stone benches surrounding the round stone-paved orchestra. By the fifth-century the stage (*skene*) consisted of a slightly raised platform and a background building. Thus the actors had three possible spaces in which to perform: the orchestra, the stage platform, and the roof of the stage building. The Chorus usually remained in the orchestra and gods tended to appear on the upper level, but any character could make use of any space during the course of a play.

According to Aristotle, it was Thespis who in the late 500s BC created this new form of pageant for the festival in honor of Dionysus. He decided to alter the traditional hymn sung by a chorus for the god, making it into a two-part song: the chorus and an individual who responded to it. This answerer was the first character of Greek drama, and his exchange with the questioning chorus was called a *dithyramb.* The opening day ceremonies had included the usual sacrifices for the god, and among these the goat, the animal sacred to Dionysus, was most prominent. The hymn sung to the god when the goat was sacrificed to him was known as the "goat-song," the *tragoidos;* this appears, then, to be the origin of the modern word tragedy.

The audience, in the morning hours probably consisting of men and women, included citizens and residents of Athens and the various nearby townships of Attica. They knew the Homeric tales and the myths upon which the plays were based, for the tragedies always retold traditional legends; it was up to each playwright to present the well-known stories in an engaging way. (19) The audience, many of whom were veterans, also knew well the hardships and suffering of war, and they recognized their own recent experiences in those stories based on events of the Trojan War.

In the early years of the fifth century Aeschylus began to write tragedies, and tradition says that he added a second actor, a second speaking part, to the existing dithyramb. His chorus numbered twelve members; at any given time two speaking actors and a chorus of twelve were on stage. Shortly after Aeschylus' initial plays Sophocles began to offer his tragedies. He added a third speaking part and increased the members of his chorus to fifteen, numbers which remained constant for the all future tragedies: three speaking parts and a fifteen-member chorus.

Professional male actors performed all the parts in the Greek tragedies, three actors per script. As there were more than three characters in the plays, each actor had to play several roles, possible because each actor wore a full-head covering mask. It was the mask which defined the character for the audience and actor alike. The costumes were elaborate and high boots made the actor seem larger, thus rendering him more visible in the large open-aired theater. Each character was identified upon entrance either in his/her own words or by an actor already on stage, so that the audience knew at once who had entered and what emotion the character had or aroused: here comes Creon and he is smiling, says Oedipus in the *Oedipus Tyrannus* (*OT* : 80-81*)* here is Antigone and I weep to see her face, the Chorus leader says as the princess comes from the palace in her play (*Ant.* 803-4).

Young men who had not yet entered upon military service made up the chorus. As each tragedy required fifteen young men, twelve more were needed for the satyr play and the comedies required twenty-four, a large number of the Athenian youth were involved in the annual festival for Dionysus. We do not know if a young man performed in one or more of the plays, but considering the difficulty of the choral songs and dances, it would seem that each chorus acted in only one play. We do know that the songs of some plays, especially those of Euripides, became the ancient equivalent of popular songs, sung beyond the day of the festival. (20)

The tragedies began in the morning; after three were performed, the morning's events closed with a satyr play. This was a short comedy, that often (but not always) included satyrs, those goat-men seen in the company of Dionysus or Pan, wanton creatures who enjoyed wine and women, song and sex. The satyr play mocked the serious themes of the tragedies, perhaps to relieve the audience of that pity and fear Aristotle would say a tragedy aroused. The four plays would be over by just before noon.

In the evening, the audience — probably only men — returned to see a comedy. While the names of several comedians are known, only those of Aristophanes, eleven of his reported forty-four scripts, remain complete. The comedies are different in form and subject: each had four speaking parts and a chorus of twenty-four, while the stories were completely original. Familiar characters from myth might appear, but the plot line was the comedian's invention. The comedies closed the days of drama, and must have ended just as the sun was setting, for each ends in some type of torch-lit event.

Thus drama as we know it today was created in fifth-century BC Greece through the writings of Aeschylus, Sophocles and Euripides in tragedy and Aristophanes in comedy. Their plays celebrated Dionysus and the myths that were part of the fabric of Athenian society. While it is true that the few plays which survive are still presented in theaters today,(21) many of these plays form the basis for new creations, new interpretations of the old stories. In the following chapters I describe Charles Mee's (re)making of seven of these ancient scripts.

Part II

Ancient Greek Drama Retold

When a contemporary playwright chooses to write a new drama based on the Greek originals, several issues come into play. Many would agree that there are only so many forms a story can take and that the archetypes developed by the Greeks are quite naturally the basis of much modern literature. Thus it is not strange that a goodly number of playwrights today turn to the ancient dramas and write versions that are, in many cases, almost direct quotations from the plays of Euripides, while others set up conflicts similar to those staged by any one of the three Athenian dramatists. In many ways, however, both the form and the inspiration of the Greek plays are different from the shows seen in theaters today. Even when the new plays are based on the ancient scripts, what is seen on stage today does not look like what was seen in the Theater of Dionysus in Athens. First, the difference in form is a difference that must be understood in two ways: the shape of the theater itself and the shape of the text.

In regard to the shape of the theater, Peter Holland has written that the action of a Greek play is tied to the acting space of the Greek theater, how Oedipus is held in place in front of his palace and within it; he does not exit the acting space. Holland continues:

> The meaning of the play is closely defined by the possibility of Oedipus's movement on, off, and across the stage. This form of tragic determinism in the actors' movement is peculiar to the most formal and formalized modes of tragedy.(22)

While we do know that some type of painted scenery was used as background on the ancient stage platform, it usually represented a palace or a temple and the first speaker on stage would identify the building and its locale. In extant dramas the only change of location during the course of the play occurs in Act III of Aeschylus' *Oresteia*, the *Eumenides*, where the action shifts from Delphi to Athens. Thus all the events of the presented story must happen in a single space; the world beyond what the audience sees can only be reported through the words of a messenger from those out-of-sight places. The world of Greek drama is entirely contained within the borders of the orchestra and its adjacent stage building, within the sacred space of the theater dedicated to Dionysus.

The written form of a Greek tragedy is also unlike the standard modern script. The ancient plays were written in iambic verse, broken by lyric interludes sung by a chorus of twelve to fifteen members; occasionally the main characters might also break into lyric meters at moments of great joy or great sorrow, expressing their deep emotions in complex poetic meters. Furthermore, as noted earlier, the number of speaking actors in the stage space was never more than three. Perhaps the fact that all actors were masked limited the number, as it would be difficult to determine who was speaking among a crowd of masked figures, but for whatever reason the greater part of a Greek script was delivered in lines designed to be said by no more than three actors, three men who changed mask and costume as their roles demanded.

The contemporary playwright need not limit the number of speaking parts, but most dramas written today do not have large casts, excluding musicals with their large choruses, if for no other than financial reasons. The writers who determine to update a Greek play must, of course, decide what to do about its chorus. If they wish to keep a certain likeness to the ancient form, they must find a way to make the chorus, that ever-present group of witnesses, an integral part of the script. The action of a modern play usually takes place in an intimate setting and any extras on stage seem out of place. The Greek plays took place entirely out of doors, both in action and in actuality, and the attendant chorus was no more out of place than it would have been in whatever "real" setting in which the action of the drama occurs. (23)

Furthermore, the modern audience expects more action than words, a lot more explicit action and far fewer words, while the idea of a hero standing forth as an example is almost bizarre. We can like the main character and perhaps identify with him (or her) but few figures in contemporary plays offer a vision of something terrible and beautiful as they face their ultimate destiny. The modern dramatists who retell the ancient stories, according to Marianne McDonald, "Call our attention to particular phenomena – war, rape, murder – but they never suggest that there is anything behind or beyond that phenomenon." (24) Thus we recognize and identify with the situation more than with any hero or heroine of the plot.

The hero of a Greek play usually learns that his destiny has caught up with him, that he has committed a terrible deed, and the audience learns his fate along with him; they do not see him do any violent action. Oedipus discovers he is the man he seeks for the murder of Laius many years ago, Heracles awakes from his madness to see what he has done while in the grip of that madness, and Hippolytus hears in his final moments that he earned his ruin because he ignored Aphrodite. In the latter play the audience did witness his scorn of the love-goddess but did not see him crash to death pursued by the bull from the sea. It is through words that the action of an ancient play takes place, usually the words of a messenger. Each person seated in the theater imagined how the scene looked and in each mental image the action of the dramas played out, meaningful to every individual in its own way. Greek drama is largely theater of the mind.

The contemporary playwright, however, cannot expect his audience to be satisfied with mere description. Although the stage does not allow the explicit violence seen in film, the modern audience is not used to listening and not seeing. A well-known example of this preference was Anthony Burgess' decision to have Oedipus blind himself on stage in the Guthrie Theatre production of 1972. Burgess described his choice in his program notes, stating that the present day audience demanded to see what happens, however bloody. The modern director, if not the playwright himself, must determine how much of the ancient non-active text can be recast for his audience, how many actions can be described but not carried out on stage. Burgess' example is perhaps extreme; the more usual practice is to have a side show of any killings, played by the actors or shown as a film clip, thus enabling the events to be seen while a messenger narrates the story.

When an ancient play is transformed for the modern world, or when a play closely tied to its own culture is translated into another language for production, the transformation and translation present both director and translator further difficulties. Despite the best efforts of both, the issue of time and distance often remain. "The past," wrote Gershon Shaked, "is a closed world unless we translate it into the present."(25) As David Johnston pointed out, while translating a play of Lope de Vega for a modern audience, some adaptation is necessary to span the distance and discrepancies between another time and one's own. "Translations and theatre are about two-way traffic," he wrote, continuing:

> [An] audience is able to experience the play as having something real and meaningful to say about the way we live our lives today, as well as allowing us to feel in some way what it must have been like to live in a time and place remote from [us.] (26)

The events that took place long ago in a world that was distant even for the fifth-century Athenian must somehow be made believable to an American audience of the current century. Perhaps that is one reason the Greek plays most often chosen for renewed production are those which deal with war. For war, its suffering and its aftermath, remain issues that seem to be forever relevant.

Then, again, there exists a difference in inspiration between the Athenian playwright and his modern counterpart. The Greeks drew their inspiration from the myths that underlay their culture, stories that were familiar to everyone in their audience. And they told their versions of the old legends as offerings to be shown in a festival for one of their most important gods. The contemporary playwrights who turn to the Greeks for their inspiration face two further problems their ancient counterparts never had to consider: the audience's unfamiliarity with the myths presented in the plays and its disbelief in the gods who so frequently directed the events portrayed. In his customary prologues, Euripides would give the first character on stage the task of laying out the story and the setting for his play. While the modern playwrights can also include such a character to narrate the story, more often they cut directly to the action, relying on program notes to explain the myth retold to the audience. If they wish to include the deities, they do not worry that their audience may not believe in them; they trust the audience to know the gods are part of the story and must be accepted on its terms. When the deities are included, they are usually present in one of two ways: either as a voice over or integrated into the modern world, appearing in a business suit or a cocktail dress. From time to time the director can play with a god's inclusion, as when David Lan, in his production of Euripides' *Ion* for the American Shakespeare Theatre Company, brought both Hermes and Athena to his stage in their customary form. Lan knew both these deities are familiar to a modern audience and the conceit worked well in his clever updating of the ancient script.

Despite the difference in form and inspiration, however, these plays still speak to an audience far removed from ancient Athens, either in direct reproductions or in modern versions, and the reason for their ability to reach a modern audience is not hard to find. The ancient stories appeal because the issues faced by the men and women on the Greek stage are the same in any time and any place and do not (often, alas) change. The situations played out by the characters in a Greek tragedy,

(27) although based on myth, remain archetypes for behavior. Wrongs done need to be in some way avenged, life and death choices must be faced, passions do run out of control, personalities warp when put in difficult circumstances. The plays which address these issues last; those that are tied too closely to a current situation win acclaim at the moment of their creation and production but do not usually survive their moment – unless a similar political or social situation arises.(28)

Charles Mee, however, has found a way to write plays that address issues both current and timeless. He has taken the old scripts and revised them to be tied to the world he sees around him: his plays unite both the ancient and the contemporary.

CHAPTER III
The Imperial Dreams Trilogy

ORESTES 2.0, AGAMEMNON 2.0, IPHIGENEIA 2.0

The three plays of Mee's *Imperial Dreams* trilogy were not composed in the myth's chronological order, any more than were those of Sophocles' "Theban Trilogy," plays grouped together but actually written over a period of some forty years.(29) Thus Mee's first (re)made Greek play was based on Euripides' *Orestes*, a late play of the Greek author and one that stands at the end of the story, while his *Iphigeneia 2.0*, whose action begins the legend, was Mee's last (re)made play of the trilogy.

The *Orestes 2.0* (1991) first played on the west coast under the direction of Robert Woodruff; it next was staged by Anne Bogart in 1992 at the Saratoga International Theatre Institute and then opened in New York in 1993 in an unusual and memorable space: an abandoned pier on the Hudson River in an En Garde Arts production under the direction of Tina Landau. *Agamemnon 2.0*, written in 1994, was first produced by the Actors' Gang in Los Angeles under the direction of Brian Kulick. Mee returned to the House of Atreus story in 2007 and *Iphigeneia 2.0* was first staged in New York that year by the Signature Theatre Company (as part of a trio of Mee plays for their fall season).

How Mee embarked upon the Greek plays came about by accident; he continued with them by conscious choice. In the fall of 1991 his long time friend Robert Woodruff, who had a chance to use the space of the Mark Taper Theater in Los Angeles, wrote to him and asked if he had anything in the works. Mee said he did not, but when Woodruff said that he was thinking about Euripides' *Orestes*, Mee agreed he'd look at the play and send out paragraphs and pages of ideas as they came to him and as relevant issues to his attention. He was attracted to the Greek play because of his own reaction to the Gulf War and the madness the military conflict was inflicting on its soldiers and the distress it was arousing in many of America's citizens. At the end of their communication, Mee says, Woodruff brought back to him this "big pile of stuff," and he reworked it into an updated version of the ancient *Orestes*.

The text now extant went through several revisions and he labeled it *2.0*, in the manner of software that goes through various versions. For Mee had decided to publish his plays on the web, making them available to all who wanted them. A published text, he has said, might sell several hundred copies at best; the website gets several million hits a year. In the following years Mee turned by choice to other ancient plays because, he says, he wanted to see drama in its clearest and cleanest form. The Greeks, he believes, wrote plays that exemplify that clarity as well as the structure which a good play requires. Mee looks back to the Greeks for what they best offer the playwright, and he continues to publish his (re) created versions on the web: ancient plays (re)told and published in a most modern form.

Mee's title for this collection of three Greek dramas, *Imperial Dreams*, refers to the House of Atreus/Agamemnon legend, centering upon the Trojan War, the events occurring before the fleet sailed to Troy, those that took place at its conclusion, and those that happened some eight years later. As a pacifist and one who stands against all wars— especially those of the first decade of the twenty-first century— Mee turns again and again to the reasons men give for going to war and the atrocities they commit during its course. He found in the Trojan War story an apt parallel for the modern attack on a Middle East nation rather near the site of ancient Troy. While the official trigger for the Greeks' attack on Priam's kingdom was Paris' abduction of Helen, the wife of Menelaus, those more concerned with economic and political causes than social and religious reasons paint a different story. Even among the ancient Greeks there circulated a legend that said Helen never went to Troy, that the war was fought for an illusion. Simonides was the first (extant) writer to put forth the alternate version, and Euripides seized upon it for his *Helen*, using it as a cover to speak against the Sicilian Expedition of 415-413 BC and show the vanity of war and the dangers of taking a military assault overseas.

ORESTES 2.0
"It's a nightmare really."

Various characters in Mee's Greek plays speak these words, but they are most prevalent in the *Orestes 2.0*. Here the nightmarish madness played out in Euripides' text is expressed in this phrase repeated six times throughout the drama: the words first appear in the script in Mee's description of the patients trapped in the military hospital where the action of the play takes place, and they are repeated by Electra, Orestes, John, and Tyndareus. The nightmare reflects and refers both to the ancient myth with its tale of murder and madness and to war as it is fought in the modern world. Whether the words refer to those images which Mee has expanded from the ancient dramatists or those he has culled from the modern world, the horror of war as it has been known and as we know it splashes across his stage.

A review of the Greek play is in order here. The *Orestes*, composed for the City Dionysia of 408 BC, is a brutal play. Euripides wrote his bitter tragedy in the late years of the long war between Athens and Sparta. The war had begun in 431 BC and was staggering to its end in 404 BC, some four years after Euripides wrote his *Orestes*. This was the final drama Euripides composed while residing in Athens; whether he was forced to leave by public pressure against his dark words or whether the downward spiral he saw in his city-state's political and moral character drove him out we cannot know. All we do know is that he journeyed north to Macedonia at the invitation of King Archelaus I. There he continued to write, sending to Athens two more plays now extant, *The Bacchae* and *Iphigeneia at Aulis*, both performed at the Theater of Dionysus during the final five years of the fifth century. Biographical legend says that Euripides died in 406 BC when attacked by the palace hounds, but as the death reports of several famous figures of antiquity are equally strange, the veracity of the story cannot be verified. As *The Bacchae* tells the tale of a mortal torn apart, many think the play influenced the biography.

Among modern critics the *Orestes* has never been considered a true tragedy; it is not a play in which the hero finds out he has taken a step toward his own ruin.(30) The plot spells out the last destructive actions carried out in the House of Atreus story. Euripides chose to tell the events immediately following those told by Aeschylus in the *Libation Bearers*, Act II of his *Oresteia* trilogy, but does not offer any such solution as does the earlier playwright's Act III, the *Eumenides*. Indeed, the plot of the *Orestes* is one of the most original in extant tragedy; its action builds around events Euripides created for his play.

The *Orestes* begins six days after Orestes has avenged the death of his father Agamemnon by killing his mother Clytemnestra. Stained with the matricide, he has been haunted by attacks of madness and remorse, but unlike in Aeschylus' version of the story, Orestes has not sought cleansing at Delphi. He has hunkered down in Mycenae where Electra, his accomplice in the deed, tends him while they both await the verdict of the Argive assembly, which is meeting this day to decide whether the siblings will be exiled or condemned to death. During the night before the play opens, Menelaus and Helen have arrived; Helen has come up to the house to be reunited with her daughter Hermione (whom Clytemnestra had been tending while Helen was in Troy) but Menelaus has stayed with his fleet down at the port of Nauplion. Electra narrates these events in her opening prologue, after which Orestes awakes in a fit of mad torment. As he sinks back to sleep a fairly irrelevant chorus of local women arrive to see what is going on, and thence the drama's action begins. One after another various relatives arrive, each of whom Orestes begs for help, none of whom agree to assist him. Helen sends a small clipping of her hair as an offering to her sister's grave but does nothing for her niece and nephew, Menelaus dithers that he has no local support, while Tyndareus (father of Helen and Clytemnestra) condemns the entire situation and vows to seek the death penalty for those who murdered his daughter.

Finally Pylades, Orestes' one and only friend, arrives and takes charge. He suggests that the two of them face the Argive assembly to plead their case. When the Argives vote their death, Pylades comes up with another plan: to take vengeance upon Menelaus before they die by killing Helen and burning the palace. Electra suggests capturing Hermione as hostage to be sure their mad scheme works. Caught in a trap and driven to desperation, the three figures respond by going on the attack. The play rises to a crescendo of impending violence with Pylades and Electra holding torches on the palace roof, Orestes holding a knife to Hermione's throat, and Menelaus shouting from down below. At this moment Apollo swings in above them all as a *deus ex machina*, with Helen accompanying on the machine, and by his directions restores the chaos to its mythic form. Violence begot madness, madness fueled dreams of vengeance, and for this ruined house only a god could restore order. Euripides, offering the corrupted House of Atreus as a paradigm for corrupted Athens, suggests that only a god could save the day — and believed that no god would come.

Mee's *Orestes 2.0* is very close to Euripides' play in both story line and text. But the setting is greatly changed: the action takes place at a seaside villa that has been transformed into a medical facility. Here the first New York staging of the *Orestes 2.0* is worth noting. Working with the En Garde Arts Company, director Tina Landau placed the villa/hospital on the old Penn Yards pier on the Hudson River at 59th street. To get to the haphazard seating, audience members had to come through a hole in the fence and make their way carefully on to the rusted site. Mee reports his own adventures in coming to see his show. "I told the cab driver," he says, "to take me to a hole in the fence of the Penn Yards construction site." But the driver refused: that is not open to the public, there is nothing there, he argued. Mee persisted, the cabbie continued to refuse. Finally Mee explained it was the site for his own play, a play based on a Greek original, a play about the ancient mythic figure Orestes. The cab driver now showed some interest: he himself was Greek. Mee reports that the driver called his dispatcher, the two nattered away in Greek, and at last the cabbie turned to him and exclaimed: "He killed his mother!" And with that he drove Mee to the hole in the fence. One never knows what will happen when the ancient Greek world comes face to face with the modern. (31)

As all the on-stage events, exits, and entrances exactly match those in the Greek original, it is easy to imagine the palace of Mycenae as part of the set, standing invisible behind the set's structure, part of that absent structure that shaped the story. Meanwhile, the insets from other characters slam the modern world into the ancient, yet leaving the ancient remains startlingly modern. The *Orestes* has always been considered a play which looks at the ways in which violence can lead to madness, and what happens when individuals refuse to recognize any responsibility for their actions.(32) Mee's (re)make of Euripides' play continues the ideas.

The characters from Euripides' play are all present on Mee's stage: Orestes, Electra, Helen, Menelaus and Pylades; even Tyndareus puts in an appearance, and Apollo arrives at the final scene. Mee creates a chorus, and although it neither sings nor dances, it is more relevant to his intent than are the women who come to visit Electra in the ancient version. Mee's chorus consists of three badly wounded veterans and three nurses who tend these wounded warriors, all of whom have seen and done terrible things in a modern war. Their interests are those of the contemporary soldier, spelling out what their Greek originals could not say. The Nurses, too, discuss their jobs and their desires. At times the lines of both Nurses and Soldiers appear to have been written more for their shock value than for any integral part of the play's theme. Mee likes to impose the modern world onto the ancient text; that is his method and his purpose. He describes his work thus:

> If we're formed by our experiences, shouldn't our work be as well? . . .
> So whether we mean to, the work we do is both received and created, both an adaptation and an original at the same time. We re-make things as we go.(33)

Although one might wonder at times exactly what the explicit and possibly offensive discussions add to the play's message, Mee's intent is to show the callous nature of much of the modern world. He took the soldiers' words from blogs posted on the web in the early years of the war and the nurses' sexual discussions from popular magazines and such writings as those of Mai Lin and other sexually extreme films and publications. All these are part of our culture, Mee argues, and have a place in a play that is about that culture, i.e., the world we really live in.

As in Euripides' play, Mee's action starts six days after Orestes has murdered Clytemnestra, six days in which he has been tormented by his deed and in which Menelaus and Helen have arrived back at Mycenae. His characterization of the two Spartans is very much that of Euripides: Helen is vain and silly, Menelaus is pompous and cowardly. For Helen, Mee has continued Euripides' comic characterization; whereas in the ancient play she is insensitive and vain, willing to give only a tiny fringe of her hair as an offering to her sister, here Mee updates her personal vanity by spelling out at some length her interest in her beauty. Menelaus, arriving later in the action, asks many questions but is repulsed by Orestes' appearance and offers no real assistance. As in the ancient play, Menelaus has no understanding of the pangs of conscience.

When Orestes first awakes, the two siblings share quiet moments of recollection and remorse; he closes the exchange with the recurring line Electra spoke at the opening of her monologue, "It's a nightmare, really." He sinks into delirious sleep and Electra remains tending him. Suddenly the telephone rings. Here Mee breaks into Euripides' play with the introduction of Farley, who exists only to speak on the phone to Electra and give her astrological advice. Mee does not banish the supernatural from his texts— Apollo will appear in the closing moments of this play— but he also likes to introduce the world beyond our own in more contemporary ways. Thus here he shows Electra as one of those who seek an answer from the conjunction of the planets, but Farley's jumbled explanations indicate that Mee inserted these lines as a parody of those who study their astrological charts.

Also extra to the modern play are the Radio Voices. Mee uses the radio device in two plays, *Orestes 2.0* and extensively in *True Love.* Here the broadcast voices speak about life elsewhere, events happening beyond the stage area. In one way, the Radio Voices function as messenger speeches, but Mee's radios report a different place, a different situation; they do not report events that have occurred off stage that effect the fate of the characters on stage. The Radio Voices offer a more subtle underlining of the plot the audience is watching unfold. The description of the other place by the Radio Voices in *Orestes 2.0* echoes that of the other life beyond the war engraved by Hephaestus on Achilles' new shield, an etching reported by Homer in Book XVIII of his *Iliad.* As Homer's words take his audience to a world not torn by war, so Mee's Radio Voices show another option to the horrors of war described by the three wounded veterans. In *Orestes 2.0* the Radio Voices describe an escape to a seaside where there exists only a place for the peaceful enjoyment of a native ambiance. But such a world is not here, and the Voices are silenced by such sounds of war as rocked the theater at the opening of the play.

The martial drum-roll marks the entrance of Menelaus, returning victorious from the conquest of Troy. Mee wants his audience to remember this is his (re)created version of an ancient play — perhaps Farley and the Radio Voices have suggested otherwise — so he clarifies his intent in his stage directions:

> Enormous cheers and a riot of static. Menelaus enters. A man
> in a trench coat enters with him, stands at a distance, moves
> occasionally to be not too distant from him. Once again, there

is a formality here, an archaic manner if not language, that is a ruined remnant of the classical world.

The flashback to the ancient world at Menelaus' entrance is a clever touch, showing how well Mee knows the ancient text(s). In Aeschylus' *Agamemnon* the king had entered on the ominous closing words of the choral song (782), "…and Justice steers all things to fulfillment." In Euripides' *Orestes*, the Spartan king is also heralded with telling words (351), "(one who is) sprung from the blood of Tantalus."

Barely has Menelaus spoken his first words when Tapemouth Man breaks free of his bonds and begins to catalogue the names of those who have been violently killed. His descriptions are not that much different from those given by Homer in various lines of his *Iliad*. The importance of the catalogue, which here, as in Homer, includes name and manner of death, is discussed in detail by Elaine Scarry in her study *The Body in Pain*. Here, as in Homer, Scarry argues, "The litany of war deaths occurs in the same way… War is not names but names, bodies and embodied culture."(34) Tapemouth Man represents a body in pain and his mistreatment is analogous to that often given to people whose wounds make them inconvenient; the ancient myth of Philoctetes comes to mind. (35) Here his words distress Menelaus and the speaker's mouth is quickly re-taped. After this brief interruption, the script returns to that of Euripides as Menelaus sees Orestes and steps back in horror at his appearance and fails to understand his nephew's crisis of conscience.

On his ancient cue Tyndareus, father of Clytemnestra, enters and begins to berate Orestes for his deed. Mee, true to form, gives the ancient Spartan a much longer speech, allowing him to wander off context to talk about the use of words and how language can have different meanings in different situations. But he returns to his point: murder, whatever name it is called, cannot be something else. Nor does he condone Menelaus' deeds at Troy. In the words of the king of Greece's most militant state Mee puts forth his own view of war and its atrocities.

Orestes, matricide that he is, now proves the accuracy of his grandfather's digression. For Mee's character, as that of Euripides, begins to justify his actions. His speech has always been a surprising example of word-turning. Indeed, from the lines of Tyndareus through the following arguments in this bitter play, the words and actions of Orestes, Pylades and Electra exemplify the well-known passage by Thucydides at Book III.82 of his *History*:

> The meaning of words had no longer the same relations to things, but was changed by them as they thought proper. Reckless daring was held to be loyal courage; prudent delay was the excuse of a coward; moderation was the disguise of unmanly weakness. . .
>
> The seal of good faith was not divine law but fellowship in crime. Revenge was dearer than self-preservation.

Thus here Orestes argues that by killing Clytemnestra he had freed the world of an example of a bad woman, a woman who took a lover and killed her husband. So Euripides' Orestes had argued; Mee's young man, of course, amplifies the reasons why he should be hailed as a hero, "forgiven and rewarded for what I've done."

Despite Orestes' clever word-play arguments, Menelaus tells his nephew that he cannot really help him; his refusal is not surprising: Helen's husband has always been a man of little action. His position is backed by one of the patients, William, sitting up and speaking for the first time to describe the conditions in the military camp. He closes his speech with the play's defining line, "It's a nightmare, really."

Before Pylades enters to assist Orestes in his attempt to influence the jury, Farley calls again and gives some further astrological advice. While he adds little to the play's action, his words serve to foreshadow how Orestes and Pylades will fail when they speak before the Argive assembly. Here again Mee returns to his ancient script and lifts almost verbatim the lines spoken by Pylades and Orestes in Euripides' drama.

In the 408 BC play, the trial before the Argive assembly is reported by a messenger; the ancient dramatist could not change the location of the action nor employ all who spoke at the legal event. Mee offers something that combines the old and the new. Before Orestes leaves for his moment in court, for which the Nurses bath and dress him, Tapemouth breaks out of his bonds again and puts forth truisms of war: (36)

> And what is remembered in the body is well remembered, and quietly displayed across the surviving generations. The record of the war survives in the bodies, both alive and buried, of the people who were hurt there--just as, from day to day, the nation is embodied in the gestures and the postures, the customs and behavior of its citizens.

The action then develops on two planes: that in the foreground is what we hear and see and is personal, that in the background is the public spectacle. Mee writes:

> During the Trial, there are two levels of text: one delivered in the foreground, one in the background, sometimes simultaneously. The foreground text, which is mostly what we hear, is all about private —indeed, intimate— life. The background text, which we mostly don't hear, is the text of public life, the trial—which is treated as so irrelevant that even those speaking it sometimes neglect to listen to it. In short, the judicial system is in ruins.

One of Euripides' most telling points about the trial in his play is that the justice system, whose origin was celebrated so gloriously by Aeschylus in the third play of his *Oresteia* trilogy in 458 BC is now corrupted, very much as that court system was failing in 408 BC Athens. Mee has understood Euripides' message well. Except, of course, the foreground words, spoken by the Nurses "as if on a radio talk show" are vulgar, entirely and obsessively about sex. Euripides' words form the background that the audience hears only intermittently and at a distance, words introduced by Tyndareus repeating the mantra of this play, "It's a nightmare really." The speeches from the trial, as reported by Euripides' messenger, are here intermixed with words from Nod and John, two of the wounded soldiers.

These two form the bridge between the two realms, as they also interact with the Nurses; it is through them that ancient and modern are united.

Madness overtakes the condemned trio in the ancient play in the ensuing scenes. Mee foretells this insanity through his three soldiers, who abuse (or kill) Tapemouth Man for no good reason; Tapemouth's fate is left up to the cast or director. For he writes in his stage directions: "When John and William turn away to go back to their places, Nod kicks the Tapemouth Man in the head three times, or shoots him in the head." Mee frequently gives alternative stage directions in his plays, either in the action or the music, for the final form of the play is not as important to him as its message. He also likes to leave the nature of the play's message up to the director, "how it feels right to him." (37)

As the characters face their court-determined death each one expresses the fear and disappointment coming upon them. Electra thinks about how much she has missed and that, although she has thought about death, she never expected it so soon. Orestes is more practical: our only choice is how we will die. When (as in Euripides' play) Electra asks him to kill her he refuses to do so: he is still stained from his mother's blood and cannot also have his sister's on his hands. As the scene progresses, Mee tells us that both characters have lost touch with reality; while Electra will fade back into their situation, Orestes "remains out of it to the end." At this point Mee returns his script to that of Euripides, allowing the action to accelerate as Pylades takes charge. He recognizes the situation and after arguing that Menelaus could have put forth a plea to save Electra at least, Pylades proposes taking down the Spartan king with them. To do so he proposes cutting Helen's throat – after all, she was the original cause of all their suffering.

And then he points out they do not have to die: they can force Menelaus to release them by taking Hermione captive. While in the ancient play it is Electra who proposes this plan, here Pylades takes over all the planning, and Electra quickly seconds his ideas. She seeks to persuade her brother by arguing that Pylades is "a person who knows the world and how it works. A person you can count on." After a few moments, Orestes agrees. Silence falls upon the stage as they exit.

In Euripides' play, the three had prayed to Zeus to assist their plan, a short prayer that seems to parody the long invocation of gods both Olympian and Chthonian in Aeschylus' *Libation Bearers*. Mee's characters offer no prayers, but he recalls the need Aeschylus had recognized. Thus as we await the outcome of the trio's plan the soldiers quietly discuss whether or not forgiveness is possible, how they can come to accept terrible deeds they have done:

WILLIAM
Do you think forgiveness is possible?
JOHN
    Uh, primarily, uh, uh, the, uh, the...primarily the question is does man have the power to forgive himself. And he does. That's essentially it. I mean if you forgive yourself, and you absolve yourself of all, uh, of all wrongdoing in an incident, then you're forgiven. Who cares what other people think.

John continues, speaking at length of the clarity that comes in his moments of madness, expressing the agony of PTSD that so many soldiers feel upon their return to civilian life.

Their discussion wanders on for a while on unimportant topics. Structurally this whole passage is the modern equivalent of the choral song that divides the action in any ancient play. We await, of course, a cry from inside the palace, and a messenger to appear and report Helen's death. A messenger does appear; he is one of Euripides' finest creations and Mee (re)creates him exactly. The Phrygian slave had (and does) report how the attack began—and how it went so completely wrong. During his description smoke begins to fill the stage: the trio is at least carrying out their plan to burn the palace. The attack on Helen failed because, while Orestes and Pylades grabbed Hermione, Helen suddenly vanished. Here first is Mee's text, then that of Euripides:

Mee: Vanished.
          They turned around
          she was gone.
          As though she
          passed right through the roof.
          And she was gone.
          As though
          stolen by the gods.
          The cause of war--
          has been removed--
          is gone--
          And all that's left--
          is ruin.

Euripides: Then they turned again
          to slaughter Zeus' daughter. But Helen
          had vanished from the room—right through the house—
          O Zeus, and earth, and light, and darkness—
          either by magic spells or wizard's skill
          or god's deceit! What happened after that
          I've no idea. Just like a fugitive,
          my legs crept from the house. So Menelaus,
          after going through such painful, painful toil,
          got his wife Helen out of Troy in vain. (1493-1502)

The soldiers pay no attention to this startling report, the failed attempt apparently makes no impression on them. Their "choral interjection," indeed, is rather an odd account of a former patient who made masks from old skulls, an action as inappropriate, perhaps, as that planned by the anger-crazed trio. The stage action resumes as Menelaus rushes in and begins to assault the doors, then to barter with Orestes on the roof. The three principles, with Hermione as hostage, threaten to burn the palace unless Menelaus allows them to live. While their lines are marked with more expletives than those of the ancient figures the dialogue otherwise follows verbatim the earlier exchange.

And then Mee's *deus ex machina* appears. Apollo had arrived via the crane on Euripides' stage; here he arrives by police helicopter. It is a perfect update. Apollo's voice comes over the loudspeaker, telling everyone to be calm.

All right.
That's enough.
Everyone stay calm.
This is Apollo speaking.

Of course his arrival is unexpected—the ancient playwrights, and Euripides in particular, liked to use the *deus ex machina* to resolve impossible scenes—at times, indeed, the playwrights seemed to deliberately create scenes that called for a divinity's hand. (38) But the sudden arrival of a god is no more unrealistic than the sudden arrival of the hero, the police squad, or the sharp shooter in nearly every contemporary movie and TV drama. One of the best examples on stage is, of course, the officer who brings pardon and the last moment reprieve in Bertolt Brecht / Kurt Weil's *Threepenny Opera*. In *Orestes 2.0* Apollo arrives, and the "deity" is Mee's final and most pointed statement about the madness that has informed this story from its very beginning. The god is dressed in a conservative business suit, and speaks quietly through a microphone, "in the manner and accent of the current American president, and his voice still fills the theatre."

Here, too, Helen is present. In antiquity she had been "asterized," turned into a star to guide sailors across the sea. Mee's Helen is "in the form of a giant blow-up fuck-me doll." The transformation is not surprising; we have come to expect explicit (and often gratuitous) sexuality from Mee. Helen, well known as the most beautiful woman in the world, has long been a sex symbol in various forms.(39) She may appear as a blow-up doll, but Apollo describes her exactly as did his ancient counterpart: she is to be a star, forever guiding mariners to their destination. However she is transformed, Helen remains an alluring and inspiring figure.

After handing out the mythic resolutions, the deity makes a speech relevant to the modern world:

This is a land whose citizens have always believed,
and still believe today, that they have a heritage,
they have a civilization and a culture,
a set of practices and well known customs
values and ideals
that are the rightful envy of the world.
This is what I believe.
The traditions that help them make a world that will endure
as long as their faith and their goodwill remain intact
and they share their gifts with all those in the world born less
fortunate than they.

Then may we say with confidence truly this is a blessed people, the rightful envy of the world.

Beautiful words, but in this context and with the action that follows, we know Mee writes them with irony and with sorrow. For after these lines, Apollo falls quiet. His bodyguards carry him out like a piece of discarded furniture. He is, of course, irrelevant. The way in which the ancient deity put the pieces back into the mythic box has never been believable and Mee's directions underline this impossibility.

Music fills the stage while the palace burns. For in *Orestes 2.0*, the god does not stop the destruction: the trio does burn down the palace. As the smoke rises, the chorus, as in any Greek play, closes the action: first the Nurses tend the dressings of the soldiers, and then the men speak out against war as they have seen it, war as they have done it. William's final lines sum it up:

We've done a lot of violence to the snivelling tendencies in our natures.
What we need now are some strong, straightforward actions that
you'd have to be a fool not to learn the wrong lessons from it . . .

Every man must shout:
there's a great destructive work to be done.
We're doing it!

In his *Orestes 2.0* Mee has followed the ancient plot line directly and the lines of Euripides' characters are frequently taken virtually verbatim from his text. Mee's play becomes a modern version through the additions of the chorus of nurses and patients and the occasional characters: the forensic expert, the Radio Voices, and the policeman/astrologist Farley. The play forces us to ask what message is intended here and for what purpose this story has been retold. What can the modern *Orestes 2.0* tell us about the issues an audience faces today?

Orestes 2.0 presents a world very much like that of 408 BC Athens: Mee's characters live in a world marked by long years of war, governmental chaos, individuals who take violence into their own hands and deny that their deeds are wrong. Torture is a theme that runs throughout Mee's script, as both the ancient characters, Electra and Orestes, and the modern additions, Nod and John, talk about their own experiences and what they have heard about from others. Mee is always an historian, and in his plays he asks his audience to remember those aspects of the past that are forever present. Perhaps that remembrance will compel people to stand up against the madness that surrounds them. But Mee knows, as Euripides did, that only the very few will understand what they need to do. Modern tragedy is not intended to bring the audience to tears in sympathy for the suffering its characters undergo. The tears come because the madness and suffering do not end. In Euripides' *Orestes* Apollo appeared to halt the madness – although it is highly doubtful that the playwright believed the gods still intervened in the violent acts of mortals. Mee's play allows the ruin to take place: neither god nor man can help a world so broken as that he sees around him. Meanwhile, the world remains a nightmare.

AGAMEMNON 2.0
"The capacity to remember"

The first play of Aeschylus' *Oresteia* trilogy and the second play of Charles Mee's *Imperial Dreams* trilogy tell the story of Agamemnon's triumphant return from the war at Troy to meet a grim death at the hands of his wife Clytemnestra. Mee's *Agamemnon* 2.0 was first produced by the Actor's Gang in Los Angeles in 1994 under the direction of Brian Kulick. It was presented together with his *Orestes 2.0* and Ellen McLaughlin's *Electra* in a program titled *The Oresteia*.(40)

Before discussing Mee's play (re)making of the play, a brief review of the myth and Aeschylus' *Agamemnon* is in order. Set at Mycenae ten years after Agamemnon has set sail for Troy, the play opens on the day Troy has fallen and in due time the conquering king arrives at his palace. While he was away his queen, Clytemnestra, plotted to take revenge on the man who sacrificed their daughter to lead the troops to war. She has sent their son Orestes away "for his own safety," kept her grieving daughter Electra in virtual servitude, and taken up with her cousin Aigisthus. The latter has his own reasons for seducing Clytemnestra: it was Agamemnon's father Atreus who killed his two brothers and served them en casserole to his father Thyestes.(41)

A watchman, assigned by Clytemnestra to look for a signal fire that will report the fall of Troy, opens the play from his post atop the palace at Mycenae. When he sees the torch, the action begins. The Chorus of Argive Elders enters and in their long opening song and during the course of their further verses sing the background of the story: how Paris' abduction of Helen began the conflict between the Greeks and the Trojans, how Agamemnon chose to sacrifice his daughter to pursue the war the gods and his brother Menelaus compelled him to wage. They also set out the greater import of Aeschylus' play: what is justice and how can it be worked out by mortals in a way that will bring a lasting harmony between those on earth and those on Mt. Olympus.

Shortly after the Greek victory at Troy has been announced, Agamemnon returns —but he does not come alone. He has brought with him his spear-won bride, Cassandra, and asks Clytemnestra to treat her well. Gleeful at this new addition to the king's insensitive and hubristic behavior, Clytemnestra announces that she has prepared a welcome appropriate for the man who has laid waste Troy. In the central scene she strews his path with crimson tapestries and persuades him to enter his palace treading on the sacred red clothes. After he exits into his palace across the crimson tapestry Clytemnestra has spread before him, Cassandra arises and envisions what is happening within the house, describing in detail the axe falling upon the king, and then she knowingly enters its doors to meet her doom. Soon those great doors of the palace open to reveal Clytemnestra standing over two bodies. In bold and joyful words she reports how she took her axe to Agamemnon and Cassandra, delighting in the blood she has shed and asserting that just vengeance has at last been accomplished. At the close of her shocking boast Aegisthus enters, also proclaiming that the long-awaited day of justice has come and the play ends. This is the story as told by Aeschylus and the script that Charles Mee (re)made into the second play of his Greek trilogy, *Agamemnon 2.0.*

Mee also retells past history in his version, often placing violent juxtapositions with modern events; he tells the story through the words of the best-known Greek historians: Homer, Hesiod, Herodotus, and Thucydides. Mee's stage directions ask that these men, dressed in long gray coats be in some way mutilated: quadriplegic, double amputee, epileptic. In the production staged at the City Garage in Santa Monica, for example, director Frederique Michel chose to have them present as talking heads, selecting to attach that of Homer to a ship as a figurehead. (42) The four historians serve both as the Watchman and the Chorus of Elders of the ancient tragedy. Thus although the original cast members are replaced, their replacements are also from the ancient world and the events of Mee's play unfold as do those of Aeschylus' drama. Mee creates his new (re)made play through dialogue and stage action.

The play opens to the lines of the Historians making the past present. They recall the space around them as once open fields. Mee creates a peaceful world, an almost dreamlike space in which they variously tell their stories. Homer tells how Simonides had a villa there and during an evening party an earthquake shook the earth and all his friends died. But he remembered where they had been and could identify their bodies; from that time on, he says: "came the beginning / of mankind's desire to remember / exactly / how the world has been / at one moment or another." And from memory came poetry, books, art, things of singular beauty.

Mee then takes us back to the world of the Trojan War as told by the Greek bards and playwrights. The four Historians variously repeat the words of Aeschylus' Chorus of Elders, reviewing the events that led to the war and to the sailing of the ships to Troy. Their words are beautiful and evocative, combining both community and personal recollections. The Historians mingle many words from the great entry song of Aeschylus' Chorus of Elders but with vocabulary that works for the modern stage. His retelling of Agamemnon's dilemma, for example, presents the King's moment of choice well and comments upon it equally well:

> Hesiod: A father's love
> and his lust for power--
> this meeting place
> of tender heart
> and a love of domination:
> Murdered her.
>
> Thucydides: The power of a public man is measured
> by how much blood and treasure
> he has the authority to waste.

A few passages later Hesiod describes standing in a stone archway and sensing someone watching him; when he turns he sees a woman in black, nailed to the stones beyond. The image tempts us to consider Clytemnestra, a woman of vengeance whom Aeschylus had described as a "woman with a man's strength of heart" (*Ag.*11), but a woman who will, in time, be pinned down. Hesiod continues with lines that compellingly link past and present, whether it be the past of the Trojan War or any time a community considers its history. The words are worth quoting here:

Sometimes
when I am by myself
I carry on a dialogue
with the past,
listening carefully
for the voices of those who have left us.
I touch the stones
with their inscriptions of past fates
inscriptions partially erased
yet still discernible.
I call up the shades
these silent bodies
silent souls
so they might feed on our compassion
and I might learn the source
of our present woes.

Hesiod's words alter the dream-like atmosphere the earlier lines had created, and prepare us for the realm into which the violent actions of the *Agamemnon 2.0* now break.

Clytemnestra enters. First she reports as a dream the fire-passed message marking the conquest of Troy. She continues here as she did in Aeschylus' play with her feminine "salad dressing" description of the chaos at Troy; her words are virtually the same in both texts:

Aeschylus: Pour vinegar and oil into the same jar
    And you might say they stand apart in hostility.
    So you may hear the cries of the victors and the vanquished,
    Different as their different fortunes.   (*Ag.* 322-25)

Mee: And this is the meaning then
    of all the rest:
    that men and women run through the streets
    shouts both of happiness and of horror
    joy and sorrow mingle equally

like vinegar and oil in one cup
unreconciled.
These are Greeks and Trojans,
victors and their prey.
Falling upon one another
equal victims of their violence.

From her Aeschylean lines the queen continues with some personal contemporary memories. Present and past mingle in Mee's (re)made Greek plays. But there is more to the drama than this obvious mingling.

For Mee's *Agamemnon 2.0* is a play of memory. While his approach, at one level, lures us to recall the ancient world from which his text arises, it has a deeper importance. Aeschylus used the House of Atreus myth to suggest how men could work out a system of justice that would lay aside the need or desire for vendetta violence. His *Oresteia* offered a mythic version of the origin of the trial by jury, where citizens could determine the course of law and do so in harmony with the gods. Mee's *Agamemnon 2.0* replaces the quest for the origin of justice with a quest for the origin of common memory, how the world came to its current condition, how war has continuously broken its possible beauty. The opening lines of the Historians introduce the theme, and each character who arrives on Mee's stage adds a further piece to it, sometimes in words alone, sometimes with appropriate props. The past remembered was once beautiful, but fragile in its loveliness, for again and again war has shattered it – and continues to do so. And thus after Clytemnestra has completed the recital of her memories, a "choral passage" marks a time break in the action, a passage in which the Historians remember events they experienced on the battlefield at Troy.

A soldier-messenger from the armies arrives with a similar tale of the horrors of war, horrors he describes more fully than does Aeschylus' messenger but true to the actions of soldiers past and present, acts of cruelty which Mee, long time pacifist, long time anti-war activist, delights in reporting in all of his plays.(43) The story is set in a mythic past, but the violent and ugly military actions the characters describe are very much those of current wars; his source for many of these lines were blogs posted by soldiers in the early years of the war in Iraq.(44) Mee has given his messenger a new prop: he draws behind him a heavy bag which he opens to reveal the various mementos he has collected from the battlefield: "[he] brings out battered, dirt-encrusted gold cups and/or rusted nineteenth century wagon wheels, a broken glass of indeterminate age, and other ruined precious or not-so-precious items from various epochs." For memories are made of many things, some of value at any time, some of value only at some times. Each age, each nation, determines what is important to it, and keeps those things as its treasures.

After denying much of the violence the Historians say they had heard about the war, the soldier-messenger offers a final speech before his exit. His words describe in heart-breaking truth the thoughts and emotions of the veteran returning from any war at any time:

> And as for me, and for my friends, we're finished--
> coming home,
> stripped of whatever it was we had.
> Before, the quiet moments between battle
> were not moments of peace
> but periods of mounting tension
> anticipating their release--
> now
> there will be no release,
> just the waiting.
> Sensation is dead.
> Time rolls on--but it has lost
> whatever it had
> that was brilliant.

At this point Mee allows his Historians to comment on the vanity of war, all war, throughout the ages. Their words might seem gratuitous, but they offer a good set up for the entrance of the man who won this most recent war. Herodotus asks the question one might well ask any returning general: should one address him with pity or with praise? (45) As they await his entrance and try to decide how to greet him, they pull out an old victrola and play a section of Arvo Pärt's *Te Deum*. The Estonian composer's music is rich and slow, evoking a sense of sorrow rather than triumph. Aeschylus had brought his Agamemnon in on the Chorus' pregnant line, "Justice steers all things to fulfillment (*Ag.* 781); Mee's king steps on stage heralded by music more appropriate for a requiem than a celebration.

Mee's Agamemnon, the conquering victor, enters with the same words he spoke in Aeschylus' drama. He draws behind him a collection of trunks and trophies ("Many more spoils than the Messenger was entitled to") but Cassandra, silent in a wagon, is not visible among them. The modern Agamemnon engages in a more lengthy dialogue with the Chorus of Historians, assuring them that all the horrors of war they have heard are not really true. His denials ring hollow, however; we know that war is violent, cruel, and ugly and his words are exactly that: cruel and ugly as he reports various deeds of violence. The words of Aeschylus' King were also shocking; one did not expect a leader to describe his actions in terms of those of a beast (827-8), "a lion lapping the blood of kings." (46) The words of the ancient Agamemnon, furthermore, showed that he and his army had shown no respect for the sacred areas of Troy, that he had not honored the gods, and the Athenian audience would know that he had sealed his destiny by such wanton actions. The *Oresteia*, of course, was a play seeking to find the correct path of justice. Charles Mee, of course, had a different agenda. For although his Agamemnon reports all actions as normal for the battlefield, the king's words only intensify the negative rumors the Historians report and turn away any praise an audience might accord a military leader. After Agamemnon has offered a long list of war-time atrocities, he sums it all up easily in the phrase that is the mantra of the plays of the *Imperial Dreams* series: "It's a nightmare really."

The Carpet Scene, the powerful central scene of Aeschylus' play, unrolls in almost exactly the same way as it did on the ancient stage. (47) Clytemnestra's persuasion speech is more sexually explicit in Mee's script than in the Greek version, but as the king removes his boots to tread the red tapestries, his action initiates the same sense of doom. As Clytemnestra celebrates her husband's entry into the palace, Hesiod falls to the ground trembling in an epileptic fit; as he gathers his strength to speak he foretells that doom awaiting the king, not in a direct warning— that must come from the Trojan captive princess — but as a ghost that devours a corpse.

At this moment Cassandra bursts forth from one of the trunks and the play returns to Aeschylus' text; her words have Mee's usual graphic and lurid additions as the playwright (re)makes the original lines. As Laura Hitchcock wrote so well in her review of the City Garage production in 2006, "With her gifts of prophecy and intuition, [Cassandra] is the character Mee uses to bewail the senselessness of repetitive butchery and the deceit leaders use to impel men to kill and be killed for greed and glory." (48) When, through Cassandra's vision, Clytemnestra lifts her axe to slay the king, the words describing the murder of Agamemnon are very close to those of Aeschylus; here are Mee's lines:

> The altar is prepared
> a hunting net made ready
> the treacherous water's poured, the bath is full
> she holds him in a trap made like a gown
> despairing hands reach out
>   [Cassandra screams]
> She strikes!
> He crashes down!
> She has murdered him!
> Agamemnon is dead!

And here are those of Aeschylus:
> Oh! See! See! Protect the bull from the cow.
> Taking him in the tangling conniving robes, with
> the black horn device she strikes!
> He falls face down in the water.
> I say to you it is a treacherous murdering bath!
> I say you will see Agamemnon dead!   (*Ag.* 1125-1129 & 1246)

Before describing how Clytemnestra raises her axe, Mee's Cassandra foretells the doom that will befall Mycenae because of the Queen's deed. Nothing beautiful or good will ever be heard within its walls again. There will be no more happy memories. She claims she has seen the four horsemen of death (Mee's addition) and the deaths of children, those of Thyestes long ago and all children killed in war's violence both past and present. Mee wants his audience to understand that the horror of war has never ended. Throughout Cassandra's prophecies, however, Thucydides, the historian who should know she speaks the truth, discredits her visions. Those who cry doom, those who discredit a current military action, are never at any time believed.

The speech Mee's Clytemnestra's gives over the bodies of Agamemnon and Cassandra has direct echoes of the Greek original. Mee recognizes that the terror and awe that we feel when viewing Aeschylus' play need no changing for modern understanding. The violent cruelty of the ancient queen needs no updating, no contemporary additions. She asserts that she knows her deed was both wrong and unforgivable — but that she would do it again. Mee, however, has omitted the most startling words of Aeschylus' queen (*Ag.* 1382-1392):

> I cast my vast net, tangling around him,
> wrapping him in a robe rich in evil.
> I struck him twice and he screamed twice,
> his limbs buckled and his body came crashing down,
> and as he lay there, I struck him again, a third blow
> for Underworld Zeus, the savior of the dead.
> He collapsed, gasping out his last breath,
> his life ebbing away, spitting spurts of blood,
> which spattered down on me like the dark sanguine dew.
> and I rejoiced just as the newly sown earth rejoices,
> when Zeus sends the nourishing rain on the young crops.

After her murderous deed the ancient queen likens herself to the Great Earth Mother who blossoms when the fruitful rain falls upon her.

It is an unforgettable image and we recognize, in fear, that her stance is her undoing, these are the words that ring her doom. For when mortals liken themselves to the gods, it is an act of hubris, and hubris in the Greek world is the deed that inevitably brings down the vengeance of the gods.

After the queen has exchanged a few lines with Thucydides, Aegisthus enters. His lines, again, are almost directly from the ancient script; Mee "updates" the role with costume and stage directions: the opportunist seducer wears only a sheet and a helmet. Aegisthus is the bedroom warrior, the man who speaks words of violence but gains his goal through seduction. The modern Aegisthus is described here as a "gigolo and homicidal maniac." He speaks lines that Mee in his stage directions says are "history as vitriol, history as vengefulness." After venting his anger against those who had wronged him and his family, Aegisthus invites Clytemnestra into the palace and into his bed and they exit to his explicit sexual invitation, an invitation Mee describes as both tender and pornographic. Mee's change in the final scene here is important: it is the usurping lover who has the last word, not the queen who wielded the axe in what she explained as proper justice, and that change alters the play from one in which the larger theme is justice to one in which the sexuality and brutality are key ideas.

But the playwright realized that these are not the major issues one should take from the ancient text (re)written. Thus he gave Hesiod a final monologue. The ancient poet / epileptic soldier comments on what has transpired and tries to connect the modern play to its ancient original, to the ideas that have made Aeschylus' play forever moving and meaningful. His words sum up Mee's theme for his (re)made play: the origin of common memory:

> This is the riddle of time:
> the human capacity to achieve remembrance
> is the capacity to transform time
> into eternity.
> Nothing human is forever;

everything perishes;
except the human heart
that has the capacity to remember
and the capacity to say:
never again
or forever.

The final statement lies at the heart of Mee's (re)making project. We must remember the past. The events from the ancient stories should teach us that such deeds as war and its horror, infidelity and its pain, vengeance and its cruelty, should never be repeated. But the very fact that these three themes can be told over and over again, updated with bits of modernity but with the ancient story still visible, shows that such deeds go on forever. Mee understands the world cannot, will not change, but he hopes that through his work he can urge people to consider the option of a better world. Until then, it really is a nightmare.

IPHIGENEIA 2.0
"Pro Patria Mori"

Mee returned to the House of Atreus story in 2007 and his *Iphigeneia 2.0* was first staged in New York that year by the Signature Theatre Company (as part of a trio of Mee plays for their fall season). Again Tina Landau was the director and the play received generally favorable reviews.

Standing first in a chronological order of the mythic story, *Iphigeneia 2.0* is Mee's latest addition to the Greek (re)making project. Unlike his *Agamemnon 2.0,* which has not been selected for presentation in recent years, the *Iphigeneia 2.0* has been popular since its first staging. The reason for this is easy to find: Euripides' *Iphigeneia at Aulis* has held pride of place next to his *Trojan Women* as an anti-war play and as the years of the wars in Iraq and Afghanistan dragged on, directors, producers, and actors chose to speak out through dramas that display the suffering of war. Mee, always the pacifist and always intent to show his audience the madness of military conflict, saw in Iphigeneia's story a way to make this point yet once again. Maybe this time the message would reach the right people.

Mee's *Iphigeneia 2.0* is almost a direct echo of Euripides' play. First, then, as before, I review the action of the original Greek drama. In the *Iphigeneia at Aulis* Euripides develops into a full-length play those few lines of Aeschylus' *Oresteia* where the Chorus of Elders describe the decision Agamemnon must make at Aulis:

> Then the elder king spoke saying this,
> It is a heavy doom to disobey,
> but it is heavy, too, if I slay my child,
> the glory of my House . . .
> Which of these is without evil?
> How can I become the deserter of the fleet,
>   failing the alliance?   (*Ag.* 205-212)

According to the myth, when the fleet of 1000 ships had gathered at Aulis to sail to Troy to punish Paris for his abduction of Helen, Agamemnon in some way offended Artemis.(49) In her anger the goddess refused to allow the fleet's departure for Troy until he offered her an appropriate sacrifice, and she considered the only suitable offering the king's first- born daughter Iphigeneia. To fulfill her demand, Agamemnon lured Iphigeneia to Aulis on the pretext of marriage to Achilles; however he used the hero's name without telling him the plan. When Iphigeneia arrives with her mother, Clytemnestra, the king tries to keep his real intent secret and pretends all preparations are for the wedding. But an old servant reveals the true situation; the queen is stunned at her husband's decision and deceit while Achilles is angry that his name had been used without his permission. Both Clytemnestra and Achilles determine to face Agamemnon and demand the truth; when Iphigeneia hears it she falls in despair at her father's knees and begs him to spare her. But suddenly, after hearing her father's explanations and seeing Achilles, Iphigeneia stands forth and accepts her destiny. She argues that her life is worth little when so many men are willing to die in battle to keep Greece free. Clytemnestra does not accept her daughter's words, but Iphigeneia decks herself in her wedding attire and goes bravely to the altar. Thus ends Euripides' play.

It seems that the goddess, appeased, let the fleet set sail for Troy.

Another version (perhaps) penned later adds a messenger speech reporting that Artemis rescued the girl at the last moment, substituting a deer for the daughter; it is a version illustrated in many mosaics and vase-paintings. But whether or not the girl was spared the knife, neither Agamemnon nor Clytemnestra saw the substitution. The king went forth to war with a bitter wind and his queen awaited his return with bitter vengeance. Artemis arriving *ex machina* and saving Iphigeneia is the version Euripides had developed in his earlier play, *Iphigeneia at Tauris,* and this variant was popular in a society which did not want to admit to a virgin sacrifice, to believe that the great Trojan War was initiated with the blood of a young maiden. But it seems that in his final play, the *Iphigeneia at Aulis,* (50) Euripides did not want to say that the deity had saved the girl, that the gods would spare a society devoted to war.

Mee takes this story and uses many of Euripides' lines: if the two scripts are juxtaposed, there are numerous parallels. But the differences are what make Mee's play entirely new. He has added to his text the familiar collection of bits culled from modern culture, here stuck on most frequently through the lines of the soldiers who form a chorus that is more closely tied to the ideas of the play than Euripides' chorus of bridesmaids — although there is a second chorus of attendant maidens in this play as well. Mee's Soldier Chorus is similar to that of Michael Cacoyannis' 1977 film version of the play. Mee's soldiers also update the carnage of war from that of Troy to that of Iraq or Afghanistan, bringing realistic gore to the descriptions of battle given by Aeschylus in his *Oresteia* or by Homer in the *Iliad*. Although Clytemnestra also speaks some updated lines, she is basically the same as her Greek original. And Iphigeneia is a direct echo, from the moment she enters expressing her love for her father and her joy at seeing him, to her shock on realizing that her marriage is to be a sacrifice, to her final acceptance of her destiny and her reasons for accepting it.

While music has been a part of each play of this trilogy, in *Iphigeneia 2.0* Mee has given it even more attention. Modern Greek folk songs open the play; for these Mee offers six choices, traditional Macedonian folk songs or any of several solos by contemporary Greek singers, sad songs that will establish the mood he wants to set off the plot and underscore the action. (51) For the Iphigeneia story, despite its theme of virgin sacrifice, appears in the scripts of both Euripides and Mee as a surprisingly modern story. The heart-wrenching drama is a domestic story in a military setting, a play which puts family values against the demands of war. It thereby tests the lengths to which a man will go to fulfill his public obligations. To highlight these ideas from the very opening of the play, Mee asks that his directors choose a folk song sung by a contemporary singer, for a culture's folk songs hold within them the sorrows of its peoples.

Songs serve to underscore words and scenes as the play unfolds. Brian Nubian's *A Soldier's Story* backs the words of the Soldier Chorus. The first meeting between Iphigeneia and her father is highlighted with a folk dance, while Hadjidakis' familiar *Never on Sunday* is played during the scene between Clytemnestra and Achilles. Here the music adds a light touch to a scene as humorous in Mee's script as in Euripides' original play. Music also serves to mark mood changes in the dramatic action. After Clytemnestra has learned Agamemnon's true intent and vows to take vengeance on her husband, the Bridesmaid Chorus enters to the joyful music of Adriatica's *The Best Pupil*. And finally, when Iphigeneia goes off to her "marriage with death" Mee directs that there be "big wedding music." (52)

Mee's play opens with Euripides' Agamemnon and the Old Man, just after the king has sent the false letter to his wife and now has second thoughts about his decision to slay his daughter to enable to fleet to sail for Troy. He outlines his dilemma to his quiet listener. The Old Man here, however, must do more than just listen: it is his job to whitewash the walls and to change the stage space during the play. He is part of the background and in charge of it.

In his opening lines, Agamemnon talks about the choices a man faces and decisions he must make. Euripides' King is troubled by what he has done and wants to recall the letter, but the reasons for his changed attitude are not fully developed. In Mee's text, they are.

Agamemnon's lines echo Mee's own words written in *Playing God. Seven Fateful Moments When Great Men Met to Change the World*. In this study of seven significant moments in history, Mee considers the difficulty of knowing all the facts, of separating appearance from reality, and of the role of chance in human affairs. Problems also arise when the interdependence of events becomes evident (the principle of contingency), when men apply the wrong lessons of history to a current problem, when they ignore the fact that any decision produces both intended and unintended consequences and, finally, the distressing detail that all these factors combined still do not give an accurate picture of the world as it is or is becoming. (53) The Greek king appears to be considering these concepts as he names his fears about war and its consequences, how empires rise and fall because their leaders cannot see the full picture. In his opening monologue he spells out at length the truth of a well-intended plan gone wrong:

Sometimes [empires] are brought to ruin
by no more than the belief
that something must be done
when in truth
doing nothing would have been the better course.

While Agamemnon is speaking four soldiers variously enter and the King continues to debate his altered decision with this mini-chorus. They respond by putting forth the real issue they and the king face: can he ask others to die when he is not willing to put his own child to death. First Soldier sums it up:

If you speak of moral law:
your own ministers say
you can't ask them to send their sons to war
knowing, without fail, some of them will die,
unless you prove your equal commitment to your goal
and sacrifice one of your own children first.

Mee's Soldier voices a sentiment familiar throughout time to many individuals and families: why can a leader demand others to die when he is not sending his own offspring to battle? Modern warfare is so often directed by generals who stay safe in their camp office, indicating where they think the battles should be fought but not going out there themselves. History tells us that Alexander the Great always led the charges against his various foes and that Roman generals were similarly in the front lines. But today we frequently see the military brass in the Command Center and not in the field. Through his Soldier's words Mee asks a question many in his audience would also voice.

Mee develops the exchange between Agamemnon and his brother Menelaus. In the ancient play the second (and lesser) Atreid stands as a foil for Agamemnon's debate; his own motivations are not fully developed and his change of heart seems almost capricious. This gave Mee space to write for Menelaus up-to-date lines about the true horror of war. He is the one to introduce the extreme and almost mindless violence that exists in war, any war; it is through his words that Mee brings the ancient story to the modern world. Mee culled Menelaus' lines from those aforementioned blogs maintained by U.S. soldiers in Iraq.(54) The harsh juxtaposition jars the audience into the realization that this is not merely an old play in a new setting with new music. In each successive scene the theme of Mee's *Iphigeneia 2.0* becomes ever more clear: this is a modern anti-war play.

When a theater group wishes to speak out against the violence and sufferings of war, it will most often choose to stage Euripides' *Trojan Women*; other groups, of course, choose *Lysistrata* to bring attention to their view via comedy, not tragedy. In the post-classical world, *Trojan Women* has been offered as a play to speak about the innocent victims of war since it was first staged in the American commercial theater in 1915. (55) During the 1960s and the years of protest against the Vietnam War, *Iphigeneia at Aulis* was added to the anti-war repertory. Whereas the ancient play might have been seen as a play of tragic choice, playing out Agamemnon's dilemma and decision at Aulis, where the king must choose between army and family, between public demands and private concerns, productions of *Iphigeneia at Aulis* presented from the 1960s to the present focus on the vanity of war and the sacrifices it demands. Through the play the producer and cast can show how the rhetoric of death for one's country can overwhelm any rational thought. As Elaine Scarry writes, in summing up her discussion on the concept of dying for one's country, whatever the claim for beginning the war, what is "substantiated is the structure of war itself... which from the day it began was understood to require of both sides the acceptance of a nonreciprocal outcome." (56) Mee's *Iphigeneia 2.0* plays into this view and makes the horrors of war explicit, and equally explicit, the vanity of *dulce et decorum est pro patria mori.*

As Menelaus continues his catalogue of war's horrors, the four Soldiers intersperse their ideas, offering in turns a second listing of the simple things a solider might want, from cookies to magazines to sex toys to drugs to baby powder. They end their catalogue with a single strong demand: "Some sense of commitment from their leaders."

The catalogue, such as the one here, is a hallmark of Mee's plays. Lists of various and numerous objects of everyday life culled from equally various and numerous sources are recounted by both his major and minor characters. The catalogue is, of course, a trope familiar to any reader of Homer's texts. But they are rare in either ancient or modern dramas. The Greek chorus will often sing of several mythic examples, tales that offer a parallel to the situation on stage. The modern musical favors repetitions over lists as exemplars in their songs. In a straight drama (as opposed to a musical) the action advances more or less directly to its conclusion; few characters spend more than a brief time for a flashback or reminiscence. (57) Mee's plays, of course, hold a place between the forms of the ancient Greek text, a modern musical, and a straight drama. The catalogues help unite these three forms. They serve, first, as a new form of chorus, in that the dramatic action stops while characters suggest or recall things they like, remember, or desire. The lists serve, secondly, as a way to widen the horizon of the play, to bring more distant worlds to the stage, and to recall life before and beyond what is now before us. The random selections included in these catalogues enrich the plays in a way unique to this playwright.

The scene ends with the re-enactment of a military drill accompanied by loud martial music while Menelaus shouts out a soldier must kill "with the veil of blood over his eyes." You, Agamemnon, his brother states in closing, must go to war yourself and "set an example for your men, how they are to behave." Familiar with the words of Aeschylus and other Greek writers, we know how Agamemnon will make war after he has killed his daughter to do so.

The stage is silent for a moment and then Achilles walks in. He will be, in time, the best soldier at Troy, the hero who will kill Hector, Troy's finest warrior. He will be the hero who in the heat of battle will go on a killing spree such as Menelaus has just described. Homer reports the bloody slaying in Book twenty-two of his *Iliad*, wherein Achilles demonstrates such behavior as Jonathan Shay has recently called the *beserker* mentality.(58)

Achilles' words to Agamemnon continue the themes Mee developed in the Greek king's opening monologue. Achilles, like his ancient counterpart, objects to being used — especially without his permission. His name is not to be freely taken to advance a secret plot. He came to serve as a soldier and is angry that he has been used as bait to bring the king's daughter to the sacrifice. In his assertions of his honor Mee's Achilles sounds very much like the Euripidean character; there his words reflect those he will use at Troy when Agamemnon dishonors him by taking his favorite girl for his own prize. Honor is all to Achilles; here he speaks of it in terms of communal respect:

> Even though you may think it trivial
> nonetheless,
> your life, too, depends upon the autonomy of others
> on the best judgment,
> not coerced, not constrained,
> but freely given, of your friends.
> This is the beginning of civil society.
> On this we build a world
> where all can flourish and prosper.

On these words, Achilles, called by Homer the greatest of the Achaeans, leaves in a huff. Immediately after his departure Iphigeneia enters.

Here Iphigeneia is dressed in the latest teenage fashions, but she is otherwise as much the daddy's girl she was in Euripides' play. She is ecstatic to see her father; her joy is underscored with the music of a traditional Greek folk dance. The happy lyrics cause Iphigeneia to lead her father into a dance with her, while her accompanying bridesmaids draw the soldiers to join them. In Euripides' play the action brings domestic life into a military camp and Mee's script does the same.

After father and daughter / husband and wife have affectionately greeted each other and talked happily about the upcoming marriage, the Chorus of Bridesmaids talk about their experiences as attendants at other weddings. As the four soldiers brought the reality of contemporary war to the story, so the four young women introduce the fun of party games to the action. Their words inspire the soldiers to reflect on happier times they have known, whether at the homes of friends or on vacation on a Caribbean island. For a brief moment, this is a happy play about a happy wedding. Clytemnestra, her daughter, and the bridesmaids then dash off to prepare for the wedding —and the play crashes back to its harsh reality. Throughout the action Mee takes his audience on a rollercoaster of emotions; in the past few scenes he has taken us from the violence of war as expressed by Menelaus to the upbeat delight in life expressed by the Bridesmaids, a delight taken up by the all the men around them. This is the good life possible if peace were to prevail, if sanity would win out against the madness of war.

The Soldiers, again left alone, reflect upon the qualities of good leadership, summing up their first observations by giving the most important word as "we," the least important, "I." They continue at some length in their discussion of leadership. Mee has made this the theme of his antiwar play: all action demands good leadership, and political and military decisions require it even more. What makes Mee's play a tragedy, even more than Iphigeneia's willing death, is that despite the knowledge of all the characters, despite the hope generated in the hearts of the audience, all involved in the story know that the Trojan War will take place. And for the fleet to sail the blood of a young maiden must be spilt.

After a "big macho dance" the soldiers exit under Menelaus' leadership and Clytemnestra enters, having just learned that there were no wedding plans. To her questioning accusations Agamemnon makes up a story: the soldiers had demanded he make a sacrifice commensurate with their own. Thus has Mee removed the goddess from his text; his general is acting under the direction of no divine command. Artemis and her directives were absent from Euripides' play as well, but he knew his audience was familiar with the myth and would assume Agamemnon had been compelled to make the sacrifice to appease her. (59) The absence of a divinity from Mee's text not only makes the play more believable for the modern audience. It leaves the actions in the realm of men, men who are facing the realities of war, both its demands and its sacrifices. It allows him to underscore, yet again, the horrible compulsion that a military decision makes upon those who direct it and those who fight in it.

Agamemnon follows his confession to his wife by explaining that he now knows it was wrong, that he cannot follow through on the plan as it now stands. He explains how he came to the first decision and to his intent to recall it:

> I thought
> I need to think of what is best for greatest number
> and so I was thinking abstractly
> not personally
> in fact
> I was not thinking clearly at all then I thought
> but how can it be the common good
> if what I do is so vile in itself?
> How can such a single act
> in a general context
> still hold good?

"How can such an act still hold good?" the king asks. Mee has turned back to Aeschylus here, where the king, in his final prayer as he lifts the knife, asks that good might prevail, that his action might be for the best:

> [How can I] stain my hands, the hands of a father
> with virgin-slaughtering blood as it drenches the altar?
> Which of the two (courses) are without evil....
> What must be must be.
> May the good prevail.
> (*Ag* 209-211, 216-17)

In Aeschylus' play the next words, spoken by the Chorus of Argive Elders, define how Agamemnon will go forth to war: he "strapped on the yoke of necessity" and went forth with a mind that would dare to do anything. The Athenian playwright knew that men, even when working with the gods, become something less than human, figures who will find no shame in committing acts of atrocity.

Mee's Agamemnon, after explaining the situation to Clytemnestra, argues that she cannot leave, that the soldiers will not go home, nor will they let her go home. He and she are caught in a trap he created when he took up the command of war. She does not accept his words or his excuses. To his arguments the queen promises vengeance upon her husband if their daughter dies; she spells out how she will murder him and abuse his body, deeds we know from earlier plays that she will do.

Once again the play's mood swings. From these ugly words of ruin the action now turns to wedding preparations with the Bridesmaids dressed and dancing until Iphigeneia enters to be decked in her wedding gown. The soldiers reappear and hustle them out, leaving the stage bare for the scene where Clytemnestra meets Achilles. In Euripides' play their encounter occurs before either know the truth, but whereas humor marks the scene in the ancient play, here it is more a matter of business: Clytemnestra wants Achilles (who was not part of the plan) to help save Iphigeneia (the victim of Agamemnon's plan). The queen suggests he do this by actually marrying her daughter; Achilles argues that he can be her savior without being her husband. But Mee has not forgotten the tenor of the ancient text's encounter: he has Clytemnestra dance closely with Achilles, a dance that suggests a sexual encounter more than that of bridegroom and bride's mother. And, as noted above, *Never on Sunday* underscores the erotic tension of the scene.

When the Bridesmaids enter Clytemnestra gives them lengthy instructions about how to behave, how to focus only on Iphigeneia's wedding, to keep her attention on her day of joy. The Soldiers return improperly dressed for the occasion and cite at length an old book of proper etiquette. But before cast and audience can begin to believe that this will, indeed, be a proper wedding, the Soldiers return to the reality of war and its violence.

> I am coming for you.
> With a peaceful heart I will destroy you.
> The whites of my eyes are the last thing you will see
> before you kiss the feet of my God.

As the mood on stage turns grim, Iphigeneia enters joyous in her bridal attire and Clytemnestra finally breaks the truth to her: there will be no wedding; her father has brought her here to sacrifice her, to kill her, for the war to begin. She rushes out, followed by her mother and her maids, leaving the Soldiers, once again, to discuss the horror of war. Mee has seized every opportunity to remind his audience that this is an anti-war play. It may be tricked out in ancient myth, there may be interludes of bridal dance, but it is a play about conflict, battle, and all the terrible things war does to those who fight it. The choral exchange ends with the "old lie:" *Dulce et decorum est / Pro patria mori.*

Wedding music introduces the next scene. All members of the wedding party variously assemble and wait to see what will happen. Iphigeneia begins to speak to her father, but she does not beg for him to spare her life. That heart-breaking speech had occurred in Euripides' play earlier in the action. Mee's play has jumped to the final encounter between father and daughter. Here Iphigeneia utters her famous lines: that he must not spare a single life and thereby put so many others in jeopardy. She further argues that it is the duty of women as well as men to sacrifice for a national cause:

> You don't mean to say
> it is only men who should risk their lives for others?
> Only men should give themselves?
> Only men should be patriots?
> Only men can be heroes?
> Not women, too?

She says she cannot stay at home and lead an ordinary (boring) life. She has been trained by her father to step forward when needed and she does not want either her mother or Achilles to stand in her way. She is ready to die:

this was my destiny
and I embrace it
I grab hold of it with both hands
and I will never let it go
because I don't want to be a useless
pointless human being
when I have a chance to have had a life.

Iphigeneia exits to her destiny and, after a moment's hesitation, Agamemnon follows her. While Clytemnestra falls to the ground in grief, the Bridesmaids slowly begin to dance with the Soldiers. For a moment it looks as if the wedding celebration will take place even if the bride is absent.

Suddenly Achilles hurls a bottle of champagne at the wall and soon everyone is in a frenzy of action, throwing wine, cake, flowers, even their clothes on the floor, at the wall, at each other. The cast turns the wedding scene into a scene of chaotic destruction, hurling wine and cake against the terrible decision they have just witnessed. The chaotic wedding scene here is, in a way, a replay of that which ends *Big Love*, written some seven years (2000) earlier. There the action ended with the brides' murder of their husbands; here it must end, beyond the stage, in the murder of the bride by her father. As Mee wrote in his stage directions:

And, bit by bit,
the world descends into a big party riot murder war
the home and war fronts combined.

This is not, however, the finale of Mee's play. Into the midst of this frenzied celebration Agamemnon returns, blood-stained, bearing his dead daughter in his arms. One by one those on stage fall silent. Stark reality stills the chaos. This final scene brings home the lie which Iphigeneia claimed to believe, that it was her most noble destiny to die for the war. It also returns the story to the opening lines, wherein Agamemnon debated the reasons empires come to ruin. So long as men believe that war is a viable answer the nightmare expressed by the characters in all three plays of this trilogy will go on. Imperial dreams in any age can only lead to both personal and national ruin.

CHAPTER IV

Three Tragedies

THE BACCHAE 2.1, THE TROJAN WOMEN - A LOVE STORY, TRUE LOVE

The three dramas that make up the series of Greek-based plays that Mee terms "tragedies" were written during the years 1993 (*Bacchae 2.1*), 1995 *(Trojan Women – A Love Story)* and 2001 (*True Love*). The first two are rather closely tied to their ancient originals, although certainly not as closely as are the plays of the *Imperial Dreams* Trilogy. *True Love*, as we shall see, spins widely and wildly away from its Greek sources. The plays also mark the beginning of Mee's interest in love stories. *The Bacchae 2.1* celebrates the god of nature, yes, but also the sexuality associated with the divinity's cult. *Trojan Women - A Love Story*, starts from the end of the Trojan War, a war which began through the instigation of Aphrodite, goddess of sexual love and continues into a second story in whose plot the love goddess was also involved. Finally *True Love* puts on stage characters who discuss, from their own experience, all possible examples of love and lust.

THE BACCHAE 2.1
"There are other pleasures, too"

The Bacchae 2.1 is an odd mixture of the hauntingly beautiful and the startlingly repulsive. In its beauty it echoes and surpasses the descriptions of nature of Euripides' text, surpassing because the beauty belongs to mortals as well as to nature. The repulsive and the vulgar are at first limited to the words of Pentheus' two Aides, but soon spreads to both Pentheus and Dionysus and, finally and especially, to the Chorus of Colored Women. The shock value that can result from the explicit and violent sexuality seems almost gratuitous: can we not know the world has all parts without an emphasis on the unpleasant? Mee's play tosses us between the two realms with the reckless abandon of nature itself. Which is, of course, his purpose.

Mee wrote his take on Euripides' play in 1993; it was produced in Los Angeles at the Mark Taper Forum's Festival of New Work under the direction of Brian Kulick. The tragedy from which Mee draws his *Bacchae 2.1* was one of Euripides' last plays. The playwright had already departed from Athens and was residing at the court of the ruler of Macedonia. He died there in 406 BC; legend reports that he was torn apart by the palace hounds. As death by rending befell the king in the *Bacchae*, many suspect that the story of the play and the story of the playwright's death were blended into one. As Euripides was in his mid-to-late 70s by that time, death from natural causes seems a better explanation. (60)

Euripides' *Bacchae* seems to report the introduction of the cult of Dionysus into Greece, into Thebes in particular. Since it is now known that the worship of the god of nature and emotion dates back to Mycenaean times, i.e., to the same period as the other Olympian deities, scholars no longer think Euripides was interested in the historical fact of the cult's introduction, but rather in what the worship of this god entails and what the deity demands of his followers. We must always remember, of course, that the play was produced at the annual civic festival for Dionysus, and is the only extant tragedy to bring the god himself on stage. Indeed, he is on stage almost continually throughout the play; Dionysus initiates and directs the drama's action. Here the god both speaks the prologue, where he stands in the orchestra in the guise of a man, and then appears at the end *ex machina* above the palace, to reveal to all the deity that he is.

Before continuing with an analysis of the play, however, it is appropriate to say a few words about the god who is the focus of the rites and in whose honor the ancient play was performed. Dionysus, offspring of an illicit union between Semele, daughter of Cadmus and princess of Thebes and Zeus, king of the Olympian gods, did not enter the world by a normal birth. Semele, prompted by the ever-jealous Hera, had asked her lover to reveal to her his true form; although he did not wish to do so Zeus obeyed her request. She was at once consumed in the flames that radiated from the god of lightening, while he snatched the unborn babe from her ashes and, according to the myth, sewed the infant into his own thigh. In time Dionysus was born from the divine thigh and raised by nymphs on Mt. Nysa in the distant east. Upon reaching his maturity the deity began to establish rites that he wished to be carried out in his honor. Dionysus was the only Olympian deity born of mortal woman who was always divine, probably because the fire of Zeus burned away any mortality from his mother and the detail of his "double birth" completed his divine status.

Euripides' *Bacchae* opens when Dionysus, appearing as a mortal, enters and announces his plan: this day Pentheus, ruler of Thebes will acknowledge him; if he does not, he will learn the power of the god he denies. Dionysus has already maddened Pentheus' mother Agave and her sisters and with the other women of Thebes they have gone to the mountains to observe the god's rites under the god's compulsion.

The women who follow Dionysus by choice, the eponymous chorus of Bacchantes, dance into the orchestra and sing in praise of the god and his rituals. Those who accept this deity of nature and emotion live a life of joy away from the constraints of city or nation. Pentheus' father Cadmus joins the ancient seer Teiresias to go forth to join in honoring the god. Before they can set out, Pentheus storms in, repeating the rumors that a strange priest is introducing a dangerous new cult into his city. He mocks his father and the seer and determines to send out soldiers to bring the imposter holy man to him. With his command he takes the first step toward his doom.

Soon Dionysus is led in — a willing captive, and deity and mortal face off against each other. They are cousins by birth, although Dionysus is now divine and Pentheus needs to recognize this. He finds the god strangely attractive, but determines that he will hold the power, that he will imprison the stranger and attempts to do so. But man cannot confine god, and Dionysus soon breaks free, first having mocked and maddened Pentheus, then having destroyed his palace around him. But still the haughty king believes he can have the upper hand. And Dionysus knows he must now unleash his power against the man who denies him.

The central scene of Euripides' *Bacchae* is one of the most terrifying in extant Greek drama. For here we see a god destroy his opponent on stage, before our eyes, and without any violent act: no flash of lightning strikes Pentheus, he does not fall down in pain or sudden death. With a single sound Dionysus halts Pentheus (810) and proceeds to destroy him through temptation: would you like to see the Bacchantes on the mountain? The god slowly invades the king's psyche, making the bold warrior into a pliant transvestite. With terrible words he leads him off to Mt. Kithairon, assuring Pentheus that he, Dionysus, is the deity most gentle and most terrible to mankind (860-61).

In the interlude the chorus sings of the power of the god, what it means to live at one with nature and to be powerful through that association. (61) Soon the expected messenger returns from the mountain and tells of the god's epiphany and how he drove Agave and her attendant maenads to tear Pentheus down from his tree-top perch and tear his body limb from limb, delighting in their bloody rending.

When Agave returns with Pentheus' head on her bacchic staff (*thrysus*) and proclaims that she has killed a ravening lion, even the Bacchante chorus stand back in horror. Cadmus returns with the gathered pieces of his grandson and slowly returns Agave to sanity. Her realization of her deed stands as the most horrific recognition scene in extant Greek drama.

She must learn what she has done and live with her knowledge. In a way, Pentheus' doom may seem to be the better one.

Above this scene, painful as it is to watch, appears the god, now revealed in his true form. Without sympathy, without regret, he pronounces that his vengeance is what Pentheus and Agave deserved: they have dared to stand against his power. Only death and exile are proper punishments for those who refuse to recognize a god.

Euripides' play is not about the introduction of the cult of Dionysus into Greece. It is rather a chilling example of a lesson many rulers have not yet learned: political power cannot stand against religious belief. A government that tries to suppress its citizens' freedom to worship as they please can only expect failure. Pentheus was not the first, nor the last, to try to control his citizens' choice to accept a god. The *Bacchae* also shows, however, the dangers of total acceptance as well as total denial: moderation, even in religion, must be observed. It is not for nothing that the most common mantra of the ancient Greeks is "nothing in excess" (*meden agan*), for excess, even in belief, can only bring ruin. These are the messages of the play that Euripides sent to Athens in the last days of his life. These are the ideas that underlie Charles Mee's modern take on Euripides' *Bacchae*, although he does, of course, add much more.

Mee's play begins quietly. Dionysus enters, stepping into a pool of light, allowing the audience to see that his costume defines him as different: he wears a white pleated linen skirt, combat boots, an orange silk blouse or tunic, a cut-off woman's nylon stocking on his head, knotted at the top, holds a gold cigarette holder and has not shaved for five days. After a few moments of silence he performs the slow whirls of a dervish. When he has seen the Chorus enter, Dionysus leaves without speaking a word. By deleting the usual Euripidean prologue Mee immediately sets up his play as something unusual, something as mysterious as the divinity himself. For although Dionysus was a full member of the Olympian pantheon, he was a deity long associated with the East; through his birth site he was a foreigner amidst the other offspring of Zeus.(62) The playwright, juxtaposing the foreign with the familiar, is playing with his audience, for soon both god and king will speak the words from the ancient Greek play.

Although Charles Mee is definitely a product of the computer and electronic age, he is as complete in his stage directions as Eugene O'Neill. The latter describes the set for his *Mourning Becomes Electra*, for example, in exacting detail; we are to know that the Mannon house itself is designed to recall the masks of the ancient dramas, masks repeated in the portraits hanging on the wall when the action of the trilogy moves inside. Mee's descriptions of his sets is less detailed than O'Neill's but he is absolutely explicit in telling us how he wants his characters to look, what he wants them to represent. It is worth citing a part of his description of the *Bacchae 2.1* chorus:

> Several might be from Africa. One from the Middle East. One from South America. And there might also be one or two others, also women of color, but from Japan or China or Indonesia, or elsewhere. These women have many qualities, as we will see in the course of the piece, but all of them must, first of all, be artists: dancers, singers, operatic singers, players of musical instruments... possessed of other extraordinary and highly developed arts that they perform with such power and beauty as to break your heart with that alone. . .So they are not just women, not just third world women, not just people from the revolutionary periphery, not just artists, but Dionysian artists.

Mee also states why he wants the women to be exotic: they are to bring to the play something foreign, passions from a world apart from the play. These are women we don't know even when they are among us. By his character directions as well as by their costumes, Mee wants to stress that this play is different, unfamiliar. For Dionysus represents forces of nature with which we do not daily interact.

While dance was a part of the rituals performed for many deities, the ecstatic dance was tied particularly to those of Dionysus. Also unique to his rites was the fact that they were carried out for no other reason than for the act of celebration itself. Dionysus may have given mortals the gift of wine, but he was not propitiated so that the vines would grow. He was honored because he had given mortals a more important gift: joy itself, and his rites allowed mortals the freedom to participate in this joy. As Barbara Ehrenreich has written, "Dionysus, in contrast, was not worshipped for ulterior reasons (to increase the crops or win the war) but for the sheer joy of his rite itself. Not only does he demand and instigate; he is the ecstatic experience that defines the sacred and sets it apart from daily life."(63) As Euripides understood in his day so Mee now well recognizes what this god has given and what he demands.

Once Mee's Chorus has gathered on stage, they begin a wild and ecstatic dance, modern in its steps and solo songs but in spirit very much like the entry march (*parodos*) of Euripides' *Bacchae*. The Greek playwright gave his chorus a beautiful and joyous song to accompany their entrance dance, but Mee leaves it to his women to find their own appropriate words: "The dancers take turns with solos, while others are at the side singing and clapping. An invigorating, sensual, sexual piece, filled with intense pleasure soaring spirits, joy." Here, again, the juxtaposition of new and old is very clear: the stage action of Mee's *Bacchae 2.1* flows in a direct line from Euripides' play, leaving the words to express the difference.

In the first scene, however, Mee brings action and words together in the scene between Tiresias and Kadmos. The two ancient followers of the new god are comic on the Greek stage and they are on Mee's as well. The two men are decked out in what they think is appropriate attire for the Dionysiac rituals and they must look foolish in their garb, for Pentheus mocks them immediately upon seeing them. Mee's ancient celebrants are equally humorously pathetic, decked out in pinstripe suits with flashy ties and handkerchiefs. Their lines are clever blend of new and ancient; while Euripides' characters state their intent to celebrate and not much more, Mee's old men spell out the joys they find in the life they have and what they expect to find by participating in the rites of the new god.

It is at this point in both plays that Pentheus enters, sees the old men and at once takes them to task. His words are wonderfully typical of Mee's (re)making style: they seem to be taken directly from Euripides' text but there are many new phrases added in. The action, however, is true to the

Greek: the king berates his father, and mocks Tiresias for trying to introduce new gods and thus get more money into his cult boxes. And he makes it clear that he will not tolerate any of his citizens taking up the new religion. This is, of course, his fatal misunderstanding, fatal in that it will bring his doom: a political leader cannot tell his people what and how to worship. As noted above, the state that tries to impose its will on its inhabitants' religion is doomed. Mee was originally an historian and although he has switched to playwriting history flows through his scripts. Thus he, like Euripides, points out again and again that men (and women) cannot be told how to worship and he turns to the Greeks to show the dangers of a state's politics interfering in the beliefs of its citizens.

Pentheus is accompanied onto the stage by two Aides, as one would expect him to be. On the Greek stage the attendants are silent but on Mee's they speak — alas. For it is in the words of these two young soldiers that Mee introduces the first words of the vulgarity that he enjoys adding to his plays, his choice of language to show that these are new and modern plays.(64) As the action continues, however (and, again, alas) the sexually ugly and violent words spread from the attendants (common men) to the plays' main characters. Thus king and deity will speak the language of the citizens whom they seek to control.(65)

But before their words turn to smut Pentheus speaks lines that are remarkably beautiful. He speaks of the world that he knows and enjoys, a civilized world, marked with man's contributions to making a better life. He points out many of these to Kadmos; one passage goes thus:

> But there are other pleasures, too.
> The pleasure of a well-ordered society that guarantees us peace in our homes and in our streets. The pleasure of living not in mud huts with roofs of thatch but in buildings of marble that may take some careful planning to design, some sense of balance and harmony so that they are built to stand, some years of labor to complete, some sense of understanding to appreciate.
>
> There is the pleasure of harmonious music.

The pleasure of elegant dance.

The pleasure of uncommon food, uncommonly prepared, and served.

The pleasures of civility.

Pentheus' lines are a more expanded version of the "formulaic" Mee catalogue, for here phrases and sentences replace the list of single words. In Pentheus' list there is a vague echo of the gifts Prometheus enumerated as his gifts to mankind in Aeschylus' *Prometheus Bound* (66)

Kadmos agrees with his grandson's words and both ignore the rude and crude comments of the Aides. Having lured his grandfather into agreement Pentheus turns to Tiresias and begins to point out the dangers of what is happening in the city, how the women in the mountains are speaking against men, and the dangers of allowing such wild behavior to continue. As Euripides' Pentheus mocked the aged seer for trying to make money off yet another new cult, so does Mee's young ruler. The latter keeps his temper under control longer than does the ancient Pentheus, but Mee's play is longer and he has more time to develop his ideas. He can allow Pentheus to muse about what he has laid aside, how he is willing to admit he prefers moderation, and play some tunes on the piano in the midst of his reflections. And then suddenly the modern play jumps back to the ancient:

Go now. Go at once.
Take some men
and find this effeminate stranger who preys on our women.
Bring him to me.
We will judge him here.
[Pentheus bolts from the piano and exits as his Aides scatter in different directions.]

Kadmos and Tiresias leave for the mountain and upon their exit Dionysus is led in and Mee's play replays Euripides' confrontation of mortal king with his divine cousin. Indeed, the lines spoken by Pentheus and Dionysus echo Euripides' script almost verbatim. Both ancient and modern texts hint at the sexual attraction the mortal ruler feels for his captive – and Mee does allow this idea to be played out in greater detail. Euripidean scholarship has long discussed Pentheus' sexual repression, including his prurient interest in the rites of Dionysus and the women who pursue them, and thus Mee's (expected) expansion of the erotic undertones of this encounter follow Euripides' lead.(67) The conversation between the principle characters takes an odd turn or two but is consistent with the play's theme. The words of the Aides, however, are again crude and inappropriate. Over and again Mee seems to suggest that the minds and vocabulary of the lower classes he inserts into his plays are basically dirty. While we do not expect the language of the uneducated to match that of the (on-stage) royalty, Mee's choice to give his working class characters crude words and off-color interests is oddly at variance with his apparent intent to present a balanced view of contemporary society. Messengers in Greek tragedies have the best speeches, colorful and yes, filled with often graphic violence, but their words always retain a certain suitability, and while they are describing things off-stage they do not ever turn to the obscene.

Mee recognizes that some of his words have been ugly and disturbing, for immediately after Pentheus leaves and the Aides lead off Dionysus in chains, Mee inserts (as in an ancient tragedy) a choral interlude. But his stage directions are telling:

> We hear beautiful sitar music —very sweet—
> an antidote to what we have just seen;
> and we watch a beautiful and gentle dance of South America or Bali.

The ancient Dionysus has often been described as a "union of opposites" as he is: citizen/stranger, male/female, god/mortal, gentle/violent. So Mee's play functions as the god himself, a union and juxtaposition of opposites.

Immediately at the close of the choral dance thunder and lightning strike, the palace crumbles and Dionysus steps free from his confinement. But before Mee's *Bacchae 2.1* returns to that of Euripides, the playwright gives Dionysus a lyrical drifting monologue about the wonders of his cult. According to stage directions, the god is now wreathed in snakes, making visible on stage the images so familiar from vase paintings of the god.(68) The relationship between Dionysus and nature has always been tenuous. For while his followers play gently with young animals and even twine snakes around their hair, he and they are portrayed as dressed in fawn or tiger skins and tear apart their animal victims with their bare hands in the culminating *sparagmos* (rending) and *omophagia* (devouring) that complete the mountain rituals.

In this monologue Dionysus offers a long description of "his happiness" in words that tell every sound and movement possible in nature; it is one of the more extensive and wide-ranging of Mee's signature catalogues. The god concludes his story thus:

> When it comes my turn to meet face to face the unspeakable vision
> of the Happy Life I shall be rendered dumb.
> But the rains of my feeling will come in torrents.

And during his recitation the theater is filled with a "prolonged shower of rose petals." Mee has brought the wondrous and powerful beauty of nature to his stage and to his theater. Following the lyrical passage Mee suggests that some there be a something magical, a dance, a circling white horse, a ring of fire, "something incredibly beautiful, sensuous, amazing, and wild." After this moment of intensified beauty Pentheus returns to the stage and the play returns to Euripides' drama.

An anonymous messenger reports to the king what he and his men have seen as they spied on the bands of women on the mountainside. Mee's names his spy Tony Ulasewitz, but laying aside a few modern phrases his report sounds like that of his Greek counterpart. The women are at peace with nature and each other, but when they see the men spying on them they fly into violent rage. The men are helpless before their attack and the women rout them from the hillside. The power of the god gives power to the women; this is what most angered Euripides' Pentheus, and Mee's king responds in the same way. He will send in the army.

Between his immediate response and his active command, Mee gives him a long speech that reveals the king's inner nature. Taking up Euripides' hint of Pentheus' prurience Mee develops and exposes the king's inner desires. He breaks into his accepted text to give Pentheus words about the intense but unexpected pleasures of sex. It is an exceptionally beautiful speech about sexual joy– surpassing the best of *Cosmo's* prose – and fully appropriate for a man who envisions what must be going on among the women on the mountain. Although we know he is wrong about their activities, Mee has allowed us to see perhaps a better side of Pentheus than the sort of "peeping Tom" Euripides created for the sex-obsessed king. And as suddenly as he has introduced this speech, Mee turns back to his ancient original.

This swift intermingling of texts is what makes Mee's (re)making project so exciting. It is of course essential that the reader or viewer know the Greek versions and know them well. A few, or even extensive, program notes cannot do full justice to what Mee has (re)created. When one knows the texts of Euripides and Aeschylus and how their plots develop, Mee's changes shine forth with a startling, exciting and (usually) pleasurable intensity. The modern playwright keeps his audience ever alert, wondering when the inserted breaks will come and what they will be, and then smile with pleasure when the familiar words are once again spoken.

So here, after his steamy erotic speech Pentheus abruptly directs his Aides to bring his armor: he will go to the mountain. Dionysus continues with Euripides' words, persuading Pentheus that he must go to the mountain in disguise as a woman, an idea Pentheus only briefly rejects. And then because this is a modern play, the re-dressing or cross-dressing (Mee gives the director a choice) takes place on stage. During the costume exchange there is "gentle" music while the Aides add voice-over comments about the attributes of the black, white and red of the costumes.

The so-called "persuasion" scene in Euripides' *Bacchae* is one of the most powerful in ancient drama but Mee's updated version has somehow missed its power. He has directed attention to the costume change itself (necessarily done off-stage at the Theater of Dionysus) and the potentially erotic nature of the naked (or almost naked) figures. But what marks this scene in Euripides' play rests upon a single word, indeed a single sound, when Dionysus stops Pentheus from going for his armor (*Bacch.* 810). Then in front of the audience the deity begins the destruction of his mortal victim, not by dismemberment (that will come later on Mt. Kithairon) but by invading his psyche. It is terrifying to see the rigid ruler become pliant through the god's words, the trained Marine turn into a docile lapdog. When the Greek Pentheus stumbles into the palace, Dionysus speaks his memorable self-descriptive line: the deity most gentle and most terrible for mankind (*Bacch.* 861). And Pentheus' return to the stage, attired as a maenad and masked as a woman, gives a shock value greater than that attained by watching his on-stage redressing.(69)

Once the two men are dressed as Maenads, Pentheus comments on his costume in a manner similar to what he does in the earlier play, although here he speaks somewhat more words. Before the two leave for the mountain, however, Mee gives the god an odd and unpleasant sexually descriptive speech. Although his manner of writing is based on the premise that he can collect bits of odd interest from the many available sources, at times the additions seem almost gratuitous.(70) Throughout Mee makes it clear that he wants his audience to recognize Dionysus not only as a god of nature but also as one of sexual license, but by focusing on this part of the god he skews the balance. Furthermore, until this point in his drama he has ignored another facet of the ancient deity: Dionysus is also the god of drama and in this play, in particular, he serves as a visible stage manager of the events on stage. We know in other plays that the gods are directing the action —Aphrodite in the *Hippolytus*, for instance — but in the *Bacchae* Dionysus sets out his plan and then carries it to conclusion in full view of the audience. In Mee's script we must wait far longer for this final aspect of the deity to be included.

Mee has not, however, overlooked the fact that Dionysus is also the god who causes madness, whose chosen method of punishment is to destroy the minds of those who disobey him. His new play is suddenly transformed into a drama whose characters are certainly beyond the world as we know it. The transformation is heralded by a revelation: one of the Bacchantes strips and becomes a Satyr: woman has changed to man (or man-beast) as Pentheus changed to woman. The stage spins and, as Mee writes in his stage directions, "We enter the land of Cockaigne-- a world of extreme unfamiliarity and extreme possibility." It is a woman's world, and we might have expected scenes such as those described by the messenger from Kithairon in Euripides' play. But this is Mee's imagining, and thus the women are deliberately bizarre: some are suspended, all are costumed lasciviously and defined by colors, and all are given lines so explicitly violent and obscene that we can only wonder if this is a nightmare, not a dream. And Mee realizes his audience may well wonder what he has staged; he gives an explanation in his text and one hopes it is repeated in the program notes:

> Women lie about.
> These are the Bacchae still, but now transformed.
> This is not a world of women;
> it is a world of particular women.
> It does not represent women;
> it presents several unique women
> who do not stand for anyone else.
> It is not a utopia,
> an idyllic, cooperative, communal female world.
> It is a strange world.

In his stage directions Mee suggests that the women, as they encircle Pentheus and entice him with their words are putting on a performance for the man newly arrived in this frightening milieu. Circling their circle however is Dionysus, who continues to walk the periphery of the stage until the end of the play. Here Mee does allow the deity to play his role as god of drama: it is Dionysus, after all, who has set up this situation and will see the action to its conclusion. The scene remains bizarre, however. Mee's interpretation of women living at one with nature, as Euripides' Bacchantes did on Mt. Kithairon – as reported by the Messenger – rests more upon a discussion of a woman's developing sexuality and tastes for strange sexual pursuits than upon any harmony that can exist between women and the natural world around them. Mee knows his Euripides, of course, and even writes an exchange between three of the women about whether nature is good or not:

TATTOOED WOMAN
And anyway, is nature good?
TATTOO ARTIST
I don't think so.
TATTOOED WOMAN
There's a lot in nature that is not pretty.
LAVENDER WOMAN
That's the part I like.

Following these lines the women then return to their preferred topic of discussion, sex, and their words rise to a crescendo of sexual obscenity. And then it all stops. The world changes again and we are back to the Theban mountain and the play's action moves from Pentheus to Agave. For here, as in the Greek original, the story belongs to her.

Mee's stage directions are explicit: he wants to be sure we know where we are: in a place of beauty that will be stained by an horrific crime. He writes (before and after Agave's quiet monologue):

Afterwards there is a long silence.
a stillness, bucolic peacefulness, resolution
[softly, heartbreaking music comes up under the following dialogue.
This is the exceedingly brief moment of bucolic
utopia before the murder of Pentheus (71)

Now the women entice Pentheus by their descriptions of the beauty of nature and what they most enjoy. Their words calmly spoken replay for a modern audience the moment of the god's epiphany as described by Euripides. (72)

Silence suddenly held the upper air, the woody glade
held its leaves silent, you could not hear the cry of beasts.
(*Bacch.* 1084-85)

And then, as it was easy for Dionysus to bind Pentheus to the pine tree he has bent to the earth, so here it is easy for Agave to take her son's hand and begin to destroy him. As today's world does not turn away from seeing violence but actually demands to see it, so Agave pounds Pentheus' head to the ground at center stage. She cries out against his deception and, as he lies dying, speaks words of triumph:

Yes,
there is some deep pleasure
in killing
some quivering love of life
some sorrow
some giddiness
some solemn thought
some exhilaration
like no other.

Mee is not original in the emotion he has given Agave here nor even modern. When Clytemnestra emerges from the palace after killing Agamemnon and Cassandra, she voices her pleasure in striking down her husband and his lover (*Ag.* 1444-47). The unity of sex, violence, murder and delight is a long-noted combination and here, in this play which so celebrates these feelings and actions, Mee has given Agave fully appropriate lines.

As it fell to Cadmus to restore Agave to reason and to recognize that she had not killed a lion but her son in Euripides' play, so here, too, Kadmos is called upon to perform the same duty. When she finally looks at what she holds and collapses into her primal scream, Kadmos prays that it is all only a dream. But the nightmare is not a dream: these characters have been caught up in a drama of epic destruction. Dionysus, god of nature (and its sexuality), madness, and drama, has brought those who stand against him to ruin. His victims cannot dismiss the situation with the words so commonly spoken in the plays of the *Imperial Dreams* trilogy, "It's a nightmare, really."

And so it is Dionysus who closes the play. Mee's god does not speak from the machine; he steps to the front of the stage, wrapping a snake around his shoulders. His final words echo those of Kadmos – but the echo mocks their wish:

DIONYSUS
These human beings:
what unfathomable creatures.
In the end,
when they feel themselves suffocating,
covered over finally in a gully filled with rubble,
swallowed up by the earth,
the thought rushes up unbidden:
it's only a dream--
this is the last
hope
we have within us.

As Kadmos and Agave cling together, first the Bacchae and then the god begin to whirl – while "either black ash or rose petals" fall from above.

"Black ash or rose petals." As a choice often appears in his stage directions, I asked Charles Mee why he gave an option, if he had a preference. He replied that he wanted it to be the director's choice, how he and his cast interpreted the play.(73) Both options would work and either would underscore the meaning chosen for a particular performance. Should I be directing *The Bacchae 2.1*, my hand would hover over the ash – but rose petals would fall. For Dionysus, as god of nature, does not respond to man's decisions, to the ruin he himself has caused. Nature is non-judgmental and as Dionysus – or any Greek deity —has no deep concern for what mortals do, so we must assume here that nature does not care. One can rail against the violence of the elements but it makes no difference; one's approval or disapproval of natural events does not change the outcome. Mortals make their own destiny; by their own choices they impose a meaning upon the world around them, but that meaning does not impose or impinge upon nature or its gods.

Mee's *The Bacchae 2.1* is a long play which, during the course of its action, must be said to fulfill Aristotle's requisite for tragedy, to arouse pity and fear in the audience. These emotions are not aroused, however, by watching the ruin of a great man whose misguided deeds reverse his fortune, who fails by trying to do the right thing but is thwarted by the gods. Pentheus tried to do what others in ancient myth also attempted: to put a political curb on a religious problem, an act many have repeated throughout history and many still attempt in the present world. But Mee's *The Bacchae 2.1* brings more than a cautionary tale to the stage. Because of his various and eclectic additions he has created a frightening world of an ever-changing reality, one which catches at the heart by its beauty and repels the mind by its vulgarity. In many ways, those words could well describe the world in which we live, the world from which we watch Mee's plays. We might choose to look only at the beauty and turn away from the vulgarity, but Mee does not allow us, his audience, such an easy out. While I or others may not care for all the words he compels us to hear or to see what he puts before us, I cannot honestly deny this other world exists. Thus, again, Mee has added another piece to his creation of a new version, if not definition, of tragedy.

THE TROJAN WOMEN - A LOVE STORY
"Men are meant to DO something"

The Trojan Women - A Love Story was first produced in 1995 under the direction of Robert Woodruff by A.R.T. in Los Angeles; the following year Tina Landau did a site specific performance with En Garde Arts at the East River Park Amphitheater in New York City. Mee's play blends Euripides' *Trojan Women* and *Hecuba*, then moves to an imaginary sequence developed from Book IV of Vergil's *Aeneid*, while a few traces of Berlioz' *Les Troyens* echo throughout both acts of the play. It was Berlioz, after all, who by choosing to base his great opera, titled *Les Troyens,* on the opening books of the *Aeneid* linked the two stories together.(74) In Mee's (re)made play the Euripidean section, which Mee calls "The Prologue," replays many lines of the 415 BC play. It also includes the description of Polyxena's death as a sacrifice to Achilles with lines from the *Hecuba.* The addition plays well, for in Euripides' *Trojan Women* the young girl's death is alluded to but not described; it is just one more of the horrors Hecuba must face. Here the aged queen receives the body of her daughter to dress for the grave, a replacement on stage for the heart-rending death rituals for Astynax staged by Euripides in his *Trojan Women.* Act II of Mee's drama, "The Play" is set in Carthage, where Dido rules over an exotic spa at which women sing, dance, exercise, and talk about various sexual positions. Dido and Aeneas fall in love; although the Queen mentions a cave, their love scenes are played out in front of the Spa Women and the Trojan refugees as well as the theater audience.

First a review of the text and context of Euripides' play is, again, in order. The Athenian play is, most scholars agree, one play of a trilogy Euripides submitted for the 415 BC City Dionysia. As the playwright's requisite three dramas usually tell separate stories, this theme-connected trilogy is unusual. External references suggest that the *Trojan Women* played third in a series which began with the *Alexander,* telling of Paris' return to Troy from his abandonment on Mt. Ida and his reintegration into the palace.(75) This play was followed by the *Palamedes,* enacting Odysseus' treacherous act against his fellow Greek soldier.(76) Thus the first play showed the origin of the Trojan War, the second an event during its course, and the last the final outcome of the conflict. The three, taken together, shows how war can begin quietly and how, as it advances, it brutalizes the men who fight it until finally it destroys their women and children. With their destruction war has laid waste all shreds of basic humanity and does not allow the conquerors to stand proud in their victory.

Euripides' plays were produced in the spring of 415 BC, several months after the Athenians' cruel attack on the island of Melos. The Melians had asked to remain neutral in the conflict between Athens and Sparta, but as their history tied them more closely to Sparta, the Athenians stated that neutrality was not an option. When the islanders refused to give in, the Athenians laid siege to Melos; when they were victorious in their assault, they killed all men still living and sold the women and children into slavery.(77) While these actions were not usual in ancient warfare, the deeds shocked many of Athens' citizens, who liked to see themselves in a better light, and Euripides was, apparently, among those shocked. Thus he presented his plays, set in Troy but clearly intended to remind his fellow Athenians of the psychological cost of the war they were waging against Sparta.

At the opening of Euripides' play, Hecuba, Queen of Troy, is lying amidst the ruins of her city. She rouses herself to speak, to outline the disasters she has endured: the death of her husband, the death of many sons, but most especially the killing of Hector, and the fall of her once proud city. To this list several more will be added during the course of the play's action. The Women of Troy soon join Hecuba to await their allotment to the victorious Greeks, for the taking of "spear-won brides" was a prize regularly awarded to the soldiers who have waged and won a war. While each woman will be sent off with a Greek man, the allotments of Hecuba's daughters comprise the plot of the drama. Cassandra, the seer divinely crazed, dances in maddened joy when she learns Agamemnon, leader of the victorious Greeks, has chosen her.(78) Despite Hecuba's remonstrance, she asserts she is happy in her allotment, for she knows she will be, in part, responsible for the King's murder at the hands of his wife Clytemnestra. Next Andromache, sitting among the spoils of war loaded onto a cart, is drawn into the orchestra; she holds her young son, Astyanax, beside her. She laments her fate, but Hecuba tries to assure her daughter that life is better than death, that she can survive to raise her son to be an avenger for Troy. But that will not happen, for the Greeks have commanded that the young boy be killed before they sail for home. And while Hecuba awaits the fulfillment of that deed, she learns her daughter Polyxena has been killed at the grave of Achilles to pacify his angry ghost. Hecuba has nothing left.

Euripides breaks his catalogue of despair to show us Helen, the cause of this war, and how she is reunited with Menelaus. Before he can berate her for her betrayal and departure, Helen turns the story to her benefit, saying how she was helpless before the Goddess of Love, how she had always tried to return to him. Hecuba sees the story for the lie that it is, but Menelaus, after a bit of bluster, asserts he will take his wife home anyway and kill her back in Sparta. It is a statement no one believes.

The final scene of this drama is the most heart-rending. The broken body of Astyanax, who had been flung from the walls of Troy, is brought to Hecuba on the shield of his father Hector. Slowly and with tears the aged Queen lays out the body of her grandson for burial — that, at least, had been allowed. The child is carried off to a grave and suddenly Hecuba and the Trojan Women see that the Greeks have set the city afire: Troy will be burned to the ground, nothing will remain but the story of their ruin.

Such a story naturally appealed to Charles Mee, ardent pacifist, who took Euripides' third play as the basis for his own opening act. But he adapted it in his customary style, creating a story that reaches far beyond the fall of Troy to an event in Rome's mythic history and, through his added bits and pieces, to the contemporary world.

The dramatic action of his Prologue follows that of Euripides' play: Hecuba arises from the rubble and the gathered chorus of Trojan women. In the following series of scenes Cassandra dances forth with her prophecies foretelling Agamemnon's doom, Andromache is separated from her child and taken off to her assigned master, Neoptolemus. Talthybius is the reluctant messenger who tells all the women, citizen wives and nobility alike, what destiny awaits them. The action also includes the re-meeting of Helen and Menelaus. Here too the king tries to bluster and Helen re-seduces him with her words and wiles, words very much the same as she spoke in Euripides' script, and wiles such as she displayed in Michael Cacoyannis' 1971 film version of the *Trojan Women*.(79) At the close of the scene, Hecuba calls forth Aeneas and charges him with saving the survivors and founding a new city which will, in time, avenge the destruction of Troy. Her words are a short retelling of the early books of Vergil's *Aeneid*, wherein the Roman poet describes the fall of Troy, how Aeneas survives and sets out on a god-directed mission to establish a new city in the west. The lines are, on Mee's part, a clever segue to his next act, based on Book IV of Vergil's epic.

This, then, is the framework of Mee's *Trojan Women - A Love Story*, the scaffolding on which he builds his play and much of the ancient framework is present in the modern setting. And, again, the playwright hangs on the existing scheme of the play the usual bits and pieces he has collected from various sources; he lists these in his notes at the end.

Many of his descriptions of the horrors of war are drawn verbatim from testimonials given by survivors of the Holocaust and Hiroshima; Elaine Scarry's work, so influential on the *Orestes 2.0*, is also cited as an influence. The women of Troy give graphic descriptions of where they were when the army attacked their city. The accounts take us to very specific sites and moments; each woman was in a different place and experienced the violence in different ways. These personal narratives that Mee gives to his various women are taken from modern sources, but they also echo those Euripides gave to his chorus members in his *Hecuba*. In their song just before they join Hecuba in her vengeance against the man who betrayed her, the Chorus women, speaking in the first person, tell how they were in the bedroom with their husband, doing up their hair for bed when suddenly there was an uproar in the streets. When they turned back from the window they saw that their husband lay dead. Soon they were captured and held in tents by the shore until they would be taken off to the Greek ships as spear-won brides (*Hec.* 914-42). Mee's Chorus also repeats words from the Euripides' *Trojan Women,* where (again in the first person) the Chorus sings thus (551-60):

> I was dancing then about the palace in honor of the mountain-dwelling virgin daughter of Zeus. A bloody shout went through the city and took the citadel of Troy. Dear children clutched their mothers' robes with trembling hands. And Ares stepped forth from his hiding place.

The brutality of war should be, must be described, and Mee minces no words when he wants to spell out the nature of military carnage. The opening act of his *Trojan Women – A Love Story,* like the third play of Euripides' trilogy, fully describes how war lays waste a city and its women, and in the process destroys all vestiges of culture and compassion. It is in the words of the two attendants on Talthybius, Bill and Ray Bob, that Mee might be said to cross the line of decency. The attendants are parallel to the two Aides of Pentheus in the *Bacchae 2.1.* Through the words of these tertiary characters Mee shows the darker side of human nature. Here the two men describe both military violence and sexual violence: the two are inseparable, Mee would argue, and he compels his audience to hear tales that sicken as well as frighten.

But it is not only reports on the terrors of military assault that are added on to Mee's framework for his (re)make of the *Trojan Women's* plot, and his other sources come into play in the Love Story section of the two-part drama. Here the bits and pieces are, again, explicitly sexual; Mee turned to the *Kama Sutra* as a source and the Spa Women name a goodly number of the positions listed in its pages. While in the Prologue, as in many of Mee's plays, the sexuality is brutal, here, in the second part of his (re)made drama, his stage directions indicate that the various characters are to reminisce about sexually beautiful encounters.

Act II, or as Mee titles it, "The Play"— others have called it "The Musical" or a "ballad opera" (80)— posits the love scene between Dido and Aeneas. The original love story was told by Vergil in Book IV of his *Aeneid.* There it is one of the most compelling and sexually exciting passages of ancient literature. Aphrodite sets the stage and sends Eros to play his part, making the Carthaginian queen fall in love with the refugee Trojan. He, in turn, stands in awe of what she has done in founding Carthage, of her leadership ability in her city, and he easily takes up her invitation to have a picnic in the country and retreat to her favorite cave.

Nevertheless, despite the passion that he and Dido share, the sorrow for what he has lost always stays with him. When he had first seen the mural in the Carthaginian temple immediately upon his arrival at the city, Aeneas had expressed that sorrow in words that became famous *sunt lacrimae rerum*: "There are tears for events and mortal things/ sufferings touch the soul." (*Aen.* I.462). The mural he sees on the Carthaginian wall depicts the battles of the Trojan War, bringing home to Aeneas that the deaths of his friends and countrymen have become the stuff of history but not necessarily of achievement. Although Mee does not give these exact words to his Aeneas, the Trojan leader's responses to Dido's offer show that Mee wants his audience to remember them, or at least the emotion they express.

But Aeneas' dalliance in Carthage does not escape the notice of the gods and soon, according to Vergil's account, the Olympians send Hermes to Carthage to remind the leader of his destiny. When Dido sees his fleet sailing away, she falls into despair and rushes to her chamber to commit suicide. Her death is one more casualty added to the list of those who died because of the Trojan War: war's victims can die far outside the actual battleground of any military conflict.

A Love Story, "The Play" of Mee's *Trojan Women-A Love Story*, appears at once as very different from The Prologue and soon it will be clear it is equally different from the story as told by Vergil. Here the lines are all Mee's own, and the setting has little to do with Carthage. Indeed, according to Mee's stage directions, the setting has little to do with any reality: "This is dreamland, a world of drift, heaven." He creates a contrast between the unending suffering of The Prologue by presenting "a pastoral idyll that takes place in a sexual utopia."(81) The scene is vaguely reminiscent of a pastoral idyll, but an idyll somewhat stained by its language. Elinor Fuchs has written that Mee's characters "are subjects in whose suffering, inner conflicts, recognition, growth or resignation we are [not] invited to take an interest," and her words ring true.(82) For the playwright is never interested in character but in situation. The story is animated by the characters on stage, but their job is to tell the tale, not arouse our emotions. This, too, is what makes Mee's (re)made Greek plays close to their source: no one weeps for Oedipus, everyone weeps for his destiny.

While adding an act about love to the brutality of the war on Troy is Mee's own creation, the idea of love as part of the Trojan story actually begins in Euripides' play. In the interlude between the taking of Astyanax and the Helen-Menelaus scene, the Trojan Chorus sing about love and its varied power (840-45 / 857-8):

> Love, Love who once came to the halls of Dardanus, Love who built up Troy, uniting her in marriage with the gods. But Dawn offers no solution, despite her marriage to a Trojan prince; she looked in horror at the deadly destruction of the city. . . The love of the gods is lost to Troy.

In Mee's Carthage, Dido is black but the women of her spa are of mixed races.(83) These women form the basic chorus, while the several shell-shocked refugees and followers of Aeneas, form a secondary chorus. Mee's script here is even more free-formed than that of some of his earlier plays. The better part of the dialogue is devoted to love: that which is discussed and displayed between Dido and Aeneas and the description of various types of sexual activity in the lines spoken by the Spa Women.

The Spa Women's opening song, sung first from their various exercise machines and then directly to the audience, is the Cowboy Junkies arrangement of *Blue Moon*. It is an appropriate song for the Dido and Aeneas story, although the audience unfamiliar with the *Aeneid* may not realize this at this point in the play; those who know their Vergil will recognize that the words of the song and the outcome of the action cannot be the same and thus will want to know how – or if – Mee has altered the ending of Book IV. The Spa Women welcome the Trojan refugees, and as they lead them to the various massage tables and chairs the men gently explain what they like about women. Their words, Mee writes in his stage notes, are not to be considered lascivious but as memories of gentler days. The opening scene of The Play is both a contrast to what went before and a set-up for what will follow. From both the setting and the words exchanged between the Soldiers and the Spa Women it is clear that this is, indeed, a love story.

Dido's entrance is marked by music.(84) She enters, sees Aeneas alone and begins to sing Linda Rondstadt's arrangement of *When You Wish Upon a Star*. Again, the song itself and its final lines set the mood and begin the action:

> Like a bolt out of the blue
> fate steps in and pulls you through
> when you wish upon a star
> your dreams come true

So singing, Dido reaches out her hand and draws Aeneas into the spa, into the play, and here, more exactly, stripped and into the hot tub. From this point on, the play is about men and women, how they act in love and what they expect from it. As the scenes progress, the sexuality becomes more explicit – Mee, after all, has used the *Kama Sutra* and Geraldo's television shows as his sources for The Play. Scott Cummings describes the action of this part of the drama thus and it seems to be an accurate description:

> The romance of Dido and Aeneas "function[s] more as a bulletin board on which he pins a myriad of texts and songs that plumb the differences between men and women and examines the mysterious desire that attracts such seeming opposites to each other." (85)

As the romance between Carthaginian Queen and Trojan Refugee continues, it does seem that Aeneas will – unlike in the original story – stay with his ardent lover.

But even as the two lovers seem content and the Spa Women chorus finish singing *Dreaming My Dreams With You* (also in the Cowboy Junkies' arrangement) Mee begins his (apparent) return to the Roman original. In a moment of stillness suddenly a "miniscule sailboat crosses from one side of the stage to the other very, very slowly" behind the two lovers. The modern playwright cannot take us to Mt. Olympus and show the deities' concern with what is going on; Vergil pictured them sending Mercury winging across the waves to Carthage to remind Aeneas that his destiny lay elsewhere. Here the little boat stands in for the messenger of the gods. While the boat/god substitution is not at once clear, its meaning becomes evident as the action progresses. Mee does not show his plan at once, however, preferring to continue to hint at the forces which lie behind the obvious and fated outcome by having Dido lay out a deck of Tarot cards for Aeneas and play them out; her intent is to show their love may well be lasting.

The Tarot cards, the words of love, the many songs and dances, however, are but distractions from the real story, that Aeneas must – and will – leave Carthage. The Trojan abandons the Carthaginian queen and, according to Vergil, his departure and the curse she sends after him is the initial cause of the three Punic Wars that the Romans fought with Carthage during the several centuries of the late Republic. (86) Myth and history: as the two were united in the story of the Trojan War so they are in Roman history. Aphrodite, goddess of love, sent Paris to Sparta; Venus, her Roman version, aroused the passion of Dido and Aeneas. Mee's modern version uniquely ties the two stories together.

When Dido learns Aeneas plans to follow his destiny and keep his promises made to both gods and men, the two begin a bitter fight. Aeneas puts forth many political (and typically male) arguments of why he must act, why he must do something. Dido, sensing she has lost him, tells him to just go.

But before Aeneas takes his first step toward his destiny, Dido grabs him, drags him back into the hot tub and pushes his head into the water. The Spa Women and Veterans also fight, creating a general melee of physical violence that marks the ending of several of Mee's plays. Finally the battle ceases, Dido crawls out of the tub and the women sing, again, *When Somebody Loves You*. The irony of the song underscores the irony of the action.

A playwright might, perhaps, change the course of history for his stage, and when Aeneas does not emerge from the tub, we assume he has died.

But Mee offers his audience a surprise: soon Aeneas drags himself out of the tub, nearly dead, but still alive to fulfill his destiny. Rome will be founded. But in his script Mee offers a second stage direction: "Or else, he doesn't drag himself out of the tub and he is dead." (87) The course of history is no longer of interest to Mee. He is interested in the story, in the power of love, in settings wherein powerful women seek to control the men who would misuse them. Mee's refusal to define the ending is his response to Euripides' use of the *deus ex machina*: the final result does not matter; it is the action that gets there that is important. Euripides did not write himself into a corner but set up his plot so that a god was needed to undo what mortals had done. No one could believe that Apollo's meting out of mythic roles at the end of the *Orestes,* for example, had any relationship to the action that led up to the final moment. So at the end of Mee's *Trojan Women - A Love Story*, what happens to Aeneas and his destiny is not nearly as important as the love story which had been played out on stage. Scott Cummings sums it up well; Mee is asking, he writes, "Why would a man, having experienced sexual delight, turn and walk away?" He continues:

> Thanatos and Eros, sun and moon, hell and heaven, tragedy and pastoral – that characterize[s] the two panels of the play's diptych. What is a man? What is a woman? What is that love that draws them together but does not last? (88)

If we look at the two stories, so different in theme but so similar in origin, we can see why Mee titles his play as he does.

In both parts of this play we can see how Mee is developing a new type of tragedy for the modern world. No one can doubt that The Prologue is a tragedy, as was the Greek original, a story marked in Mee's words by the horrors of war updated from those described by Euripides. But The Play, despite its seeming beauty and its many songs, is also a tragedy, even as is Vergil's *Aeneid* IV. Both stories tell the sufferings that men create for themselves and for the women who are caught up in the actions of men. Men must act and in their determination to carry out their goals they destroy so many lives and so many opportunities for happiness.

TRUE LOVE
"Love is who you are"

Mee says that his *True Love* is based on Euripides' *Hippolytus* (and the variations by Seneca and Racine) and Plato's *Symposium*. The latter was an important book in his life. As he tells the story in his autobiography, when he was in the hospital bed recovering from the polio, his English teacher brought him a copy of Plato's work. He read it –"the first book [he] ever read"– and its impact was great. For from his teacher's gift Mee realized he would have to change the way he looked at his life; his would be a life of the mind, not the body.(89)

True Love, written in 2001 as a vehicle for his then current love Laurie Williams, stands furthest removed from his sources; unlike the other plays in his Greek (re)making project, this play takes few lines from either Euripides or Plato. Their inspiration gives the impetus for Polly's passion for her stepson, an attraction based on the Hippolytus legend, while the quest for the nature of love is based on the topic of discussion in Plato's *Symposium*. As Elyse Sommer says in her 2001 review of the play's premier performance, however, both ancient authors would be "taken aback" at what Mee has done with their work.(90)

In Euripides' *Hippolytus*, the version which the dramatist offered for the festival of Dionysus in 428 BC, Aphrodite, Goddess of Sexual Love, takes out her vengeful anger against Hippolytus for refusing to recognize her or her power while giving all his worship to the chaste goddess Artemis. Aphrodite's method is to curse the young prince's stepmother Phaedra with an overwhelming passion for him. The queen knows she must fight this passion; she struggles hard until, defeated in her attempts, she commits suicide before her lust can become known to her husband (or her stepson). Euripides had written another version of the legend a few years earlier, a version in which Phaedra lets Hippolytus know of her illicit desire.(91) In the extant text her Nurse betrays her passion to the prince and Phaedra knows she is ruined. When she overhears Hippolytus' tirade against all women (and her in particular) after he has learned of her feelings, her shame and his rejection of her passion leads her to put a noose around her neck. But she does not allow the young man to escape the outcome of his angry and arrogant words. Before Phaedra dies she writes a letter falsely accusing Hippolytus of raping her.

When her husband Theseus returns to Troizen, he finds his wife dead and reads the letter fastened to her lifeless hand. In immediate anger he curses his son and commits him to exile, and the prince cannot convince his father that he is innocent. While he is en route as an outcast to a foreign land, his team of trusted horses bolts and drags him to his death. The messenger reports how Hippolytus' chariot crashed: the horses went into a panic and dashed away when a raging bull charged from the sea. Poseidon had sent the bull in answer to Theseus' prayer to his sea-god father to destroy his apparently wanton son.(92) It is only when the young man is gasping out his life at the feet of his father that Artemis appears and tells the king the true story of Aphrodite's anger, Phaedra's lie, and how his own misguided curse had roused from the sea the bull that killed his son. The play is one of Euripides' most tragic, whether as an explication of the implacable wrath of the gods or as an example of how mortals bring about their own ruin.

The play's premise, i.e., the power and vengeance of Aphrodite, serves as a vehicle for Mee to discuss love in its many forms, both beautiful and base. The plot line may be traced, but the characters in *True Love* are far removed from the noble figures of ancient myth. The setting of the play, furthermore, seems designed to juxtapose beautiful words against a particularly banal and displeasing setting. For the action takes place in a junky gas station, complete with a broken-down car and a rusted bedstead, alongside a motel with its name remaining in only a few broken letters "Mo el Aph it." But the gas pump which stands at center stage in bright orange and yellow paint Mee describes as "surreally supremely beautiful" Perhaps Mee wanted something beautiful in his story of true love; one might also suggest that the pump, as part of the stage set, is a replacement for the deities found framing Euripides' stage. But the pump is important only as a visual image; no power is expected from it nor is worship extended to it. Standing center stage in its beauty the gas pump is as oblivious to the actions of those around it as is any Greek deity. The beauty of the pump stands in contrast to the ugliness around it, suggesting the beauty of the play's subject, love, in contrast to the many unattractive ways love is described. Words versus scene appears to be one of Mee's intents in *True Love*.

Each character, meanwhile, with the possible exception of Edward, Polly's desirable and desired teenage stepson, has some sexual fetish or has experienced rape and/or incest at some point in their past. In his quest to answer the question posed in Plato's *Symposium*, "What is love?" Mee has replaced the Greek philosophers "with a motley crew of workaday philosophers: mechanics, a slatternly girl, [and] a transvestite beautician."(93)   To each of his characters he has given at least one monologue on the various sexual options that each has experienced and (reportedly) enjoyed.

Although Mee says that the plays behind *True Love* are Euripides' *Hippolytus* and Racine's *Phaedra*, he admits that he has moved far away from these earlier scripts. He writes:

> With *True Love*, I think, my method has come unhinged and is almost spinning out of control. It is riffing galore. There's only a shred of a story line: will the stepmother seduce her stepson or not? Everything else is riff. I wanted to see how far you could stretch the container. And I think this is close to the outer limit, just this side of a play without any plot.(94)

Mee is not the first playwright to take the Hippolytus legend in a far different direction.(95)   Eugene O'Neill's *Desire Under the Elms* is also a "riff" on the story, and it, too, veers far away from the Greek original. O'Neill's play builds the story of illicit passion, allowing it to be fulfilled with tragic results. Mee's take on the legend, on the other hand, leaves the Hippolytus story as almost tangential – although the ancient play gives the shape for the modern – for his interest lies in the question raised in Plato's *Symposium*: what is love. It is worth noting, perhaps, that both takes on the ancient story perforce leave the deities out; in both O'Neill's tragic drama and Mee's study of love, all action remains in the hands of men and women.(96)   It is also worth noting that in Euripides' play, although the goddesses frame the play (and the stage), the characters deliberate and make their own choices, trying desperately to control the action. What makes his play so tragic is that with each choice a character makes he or she steps into the gods' plan.(97)

We can trace the plot and characters of the *Hippolytus* lurking behind the story line and cast of *True Love*. Polly, Mee's Phaedra, has been abandoned, albeit briefly, by Richard, and finds Edward, his son and her stepson, desirable. As this is a modern tale, she does successfully seduce him, an alliance which does not really satisfy her and turns him away. Edward's character is shadowed by that of Hippolytus in that he has had little experience of sex and shows little interest in acquiring more. He listens to radio music and finds athletic pursuits more appealing. Thus is Edward a modern Hippolytus, for his Greek original preferred to hunt and to live apart from city life. During the course of Mee's play Polly becomes ever more distracted, ever more at a loss, and her growing discomfort echoes the madness of Phaedra, whom the love goddess has driven wild with illicit desire.

Edward enters first onto the stage, then Polly. He ignores her, she silently watches him. In the original story, Phaedra had hidden behind a bush and secretly watched Hippolytus exercising; it was then that she fell in love with him and set up a sanctuary in his honor (*Hipp.* 24–33).(98) In addition to repeating the ancient myth, Mee's stage directions spell out the relationship between Polly and Edward; he wants his audience to recognize the Greek original in the opening scene and expects director and cast to make his stage directions clear. For it is important, he asserts, that the audience hold that recognition of their relationship through the chaos of the play. He writes:

> This opening moment of the piece—
> first Edward alone on stage,
> then Polly watching him,
> is meant to establish the two principals of the piece,
> and their relationship,
> so that this relationship--and plotline--

is stated clearly enough at the top of the piece
that we have noted it, attached our attention to it,
and can track it through the confusion that follows.

Although the framing deities of Euripides' play are absent, Mee replaces them, bringing in the outside world via Radio Voices. Mee had used this device earlier in *Orestes 2.0*, where Radio Voices also replaced the ancient deities. The first lines of *True Love* come from the radio, turned to a talk show about the nature of love. The radio and the subject of its talk show make a good stand-in for Aphrodite, while the theme of the talk show leads into the theme of the play, the nature of love. Mee once said about this play (and its twisted characters) words that explain the play's title: "Relationships are twisted. Any form of love is true because it's the only kind of love they— the characters — are capable of."(99)

True Love is the only Greek-based tragedy that does not take its name from the ancient character whose story shapes the plot. After giving us *Orestes 2.0, Agamemnon 2.0, Bacchae 2.1, Trojan Women - A Love Story* and *Iphigeneia 2.0*, Mee titles this last play from its subject matter, *True Love*. The title is fully appropriate, for it is a play that starts from the theme of Plato's *Symposium* and carries it to a modern extreme. Its bawdy nature is also appropriate to stand at the end of the tragic series, for at the ancient City Dionysia each of the three days of tragedy ended at noon with the racy and comic satyr play. From what we know of this last drama of the morning, the plot took a myth and retold it in a totally irreverent way. Certainly *True Love* does that.

The play, like the others, is filled with music. Sometimes Mee is specific about which song he wants used, at other times he leaves it up to the director, with stage notes that frequently only say "music" or "a love song." As noted before, at times Mee cares little about the specifics of what happens on stage (Aeneas dies, or he does not die in The Play of *Trojan Women – A Love Story*), preferring to focus on the process more than the reality of the action. The music Mee does name is, again, drawn from many sources, from the classical to the far alternative. The former is represented by Handel's "Pena Tiranna" from *Amadigi di Gaula,* "heartbreaking music," the latter is Screamin' Jay Hawkins' version of *I Put a Spell on You* (mind-breaking noise). Throughout the play the "Garage Band" assembled by the cast play country love songs or riff on whatever music has been heard on the radio. Mee loves music in all his plays, as we have seen, but here especially the lyric breaks serve several functions. First, they recall the ancient Greek fondness for music, secondly they replace the ancient chorus, and finally they emphasize the sensual experience of the play: this is a play in which the plot line is secondary to what happens on stage, what the audience sees and hears.

In this play in particular, Mee's emphasis is clearly on the words and the visual images. There is little action on stage in any ancient Greek drama— all the exciting action takes place in the words of the messenger; the major exception, as noted above, is the Carpet Scene in Aeschylus' *Agamemnon.* Mee copies his Greek originals in this manner. In his *Agamemnon 2.0* he also stages the moment the king treads on the tapestries, but in his (re)made scripts little action that advances the plot happens on stage. The dances in the *Iphigeneia 2.0* set the mood while the hot-tub scene in The Play of *Trojan Women – A Love Story* creates some suspense. The costume change in *Bacchae 2.1* does the most, perhaps, to advance the story. Euripides had costumed Pentheus as a maenad but off-stage while Mee, as noted above, is true to his method and modern expectations, and lets the audience see the action. In *True Love* we see Polly take Edward into the car but we do not see them make love.

True Love, however, rather differs from the earlier plays in that Mee has added to this "tragedy" the wild physical actions he had specified for *Big Love* the year before. These seem to be included more for excitement or shock value rather than adding anything to the story or advancing (whatever plot) there is. We watch a number of wanton dances and several times the men throw themselves to the floor for no good reason except to show physical prowess. Phil and Red Dicks, for example, engage in what Mee describes (in his stage notes) "a roughhouse" dance. They throw each other to the floor, jumping on each other; one pulls the other upright and then throws him to the ground again. During this choreographed conflict, both of them are "screaming with horror and delight as the violent dance goes on and on, neither really hurting the other."

In addition to such displays of physical energy there are bizarre and seemingly meaningless actions. At various points we see Polly with a chicken: she has it on a leash, she whirls it, throws it, and leaves it for dead — but the bird comes back to life and is tossed in the car. There is the apparently senseless sequence when Jim lights his own hands with lighter fluid. All of these peculiar and seemingly gratuitous events serve, again, to tilt *True Love* to the realm of the satyr play. The original sources, Euripides' *Hippolytus* and Plato's *Symposium*, are long forgotten in the stage activity.

The ideas from the two ancient sources do remain in the various characters' speeches. These are frequently long, as the men and women talk about the forms of love they like, the forms of love they have experienced, the forms of love which they wish they could have as their own. There are, however, probably too many words in *True Love*, for Mee has included all possible and (one could argue) impossible types of sexual alliances in the characters' discussions. There is but one example of the requisite catalogue, seemingly thrown in merely for fun and to keep the trope alive: each character suggests a lipstick color that Alicia might use.

Nevertheless, behind the wanton action and numerous (and often gratuitously shocking) words, the ancient sources remain. The *Hippolytus* reappears behind Edward's words, as he expresses his hesitation about sex and his basic dislike of being forced into a sexual world. In her long monologue on love Polly suddenly says:

And nothing could be more horrifying to a woman
than the love she may feel for someone
she can't resist--
because then she knows
suddenly she's become the unwilling subject
of the uncontrollable,
indiscriminate excitement of just pure animal sex.

Her words are an unconscious echo of Phaedra's story. Somewhat later, in the course of her breakdown, Polly cries out, "I probably should kill myself," words which recall Phaedra's madness and shame; the Greek queen, of course, does commit suicide. Richard's anger when he returns and discovers that Polly and Edward have made love recalls Theseus' rage when he reads Phaedra's false letter. The careful reader (or truly watchful audience member) can find these traces in the play and can remember Mee started from Euripides' play.

Plato's *Symposium* can also be found lurking in the script, although the story of the ancient philosophers' drinking party is less visible than the ancient drama. The strange sexual experiences that Mee's characters describe spin way beyond anything found in the Greek text. But Plato is still there. For each of his philosophers' descriptions of Love treat it both sexually and morally, speaking of the emotion directed by Aphrodite Pandemos, the goddess who looks after physical love and that aroused by Aphrodite Urania, through whom men create all good things in life. As per Greek society several of the philosophers praise homosexual love, so we find Mee's characters describing similar sexual encounters. Mee, as he himself said (see above) however, spins the possibilities way beyond what the Greeks might have suggested.

There is a further difference between the two works, between the *Symposium* and *True Love*. Plato's philosophers praise love, and, through Socrates, argue that it is through the desire of wanting something one lacks, something good, that Love draws men's souls ever upward. In Mee's play much of the love is destructive and, despite the beauty the garage residents want to find or have briefly sensed in their relationships, for them love is more a source of pain than pleasure. There is no vision of Perfect Love in Mee's text.

The ending of *True Love* is surprising and as it occurs seems senseless. After reflecting on going to a performance of Aeschylus' *Danaids* in a marble quarry(100) and listening to the beautiful music of Handel's "*Saraband* from Suite No. 11 Harpsichord," Richard shoots Polly dead and then commits suicide. But the unexpected killing is not a random choice for the ending. As their two bodies lie dead on the stage, Mee is asking his audience to recollect the two dead figures at the finale of the *Hippolytus*. In the Greek play it was Phaedra and Hippolytus, two innocent victims of divine wrath, who have died, while in the Mee (re) make it is the wife Polly (Phaedra) and the husband Richard (Theseus) who are dead, both by a single and mortal hand.

After the wild digressions Mee's (re)make of the ancient play returns to reflect the ancient script in the closing scene. As the play had opened with the Radio Talk Show about love, it ends with the Radio Talk Show telling the Hippolytus and Phaedra/ Polly and Edward story, albeit in a different context. The Radio Voices discuss a couple in upstate New York, who appear to have been doubles of the three principles in this show, who survived the events we have just seen. The woman did not die but lived with her stepson, while the husband also escaped death, if not mental deterioration, and lived in a trailer next door, working at the gas station. Although the bodies of Polly and Richard are carried off, we are left wondering if, perhaps, that upstate New York couple's story is true for Richard, Polly and Edward.

The Radio Talk Show Voices frame Mee's play as the goddesses, Aphrodite in the prologue, Artemis in the Epilogue, frame Euripides' drama. Aphrodite had set out what would happen: love and death; the opening Radio Talk Show introduced the topic of varied possibilities of love. Artemis confirmed why the tragedy unrolled as it did, and confirmed that the story of Phaedra and Hippolytus would live on in the pre-wedding rituals of young girls (*Hipp.* 1423-1430).(101) The Radio Voices suggest that the Polly and Edward story might also live on, becoming the subject of Radio Talk Shows, a modern echo, perhaps, of ancient rituals where legends are retold.

There is also a replay of the ancient *deus ex machina* in the words of the final Radio Talk Show sequence: the altered ending of the story, i.e., what was seen on stage may not be what happened. In what is usually considered to be a later addition to Euripides' last play, *Iphigeneia at Aulis*, a messenger dashes in to tell Clytemnestra that at the last moment Artemis snatched the princess from the altar and substituted a deer for the daughter. This alternative version presents a more acceptable ending to the story, allowing the Greek audience to believe the Trojan War, the great story of their past glory, was not undertaken stained by virgin blood. Euripides probably did not write that messenger speech, and, in any event, Agamemnon did not see the substitution and Clytemnestra did not regain Iphigeneia. Artemis saved the princess but whisked her off to serve as priestess of her rites among the Taurians.(102) Mee's offering of another story as the ending to his (re)make of the Greek play allows his audience to hope that true love may not end in death after all. But it is just that, a hope, for what we have seen is closer to the nightmare of the earlier tragedies.

CHAPTER V
Tragedy To Comedy
BIG LOVE
"Love Is The Highest Law"

Six years after writing *Agamemnon 2.0*, Mee returned to Aeschylus. *Big Love* premiered in March, 2000 at the Humana Festival Louisville, Kentucky, under the direction of Les Waters. It soon became Mee's most popular play, staged in theaters around the country and especially on college campuses. In a drama once considered to be the earliest Greek tragedy,(103) Mee found the source for *Big Love,* a play he terms, correctly for his version, a comedy. Starting from the tragic *Suppliant Maidens,* Mee takes the vaguely absurd legend – 49 brides slaying 49 husbands on their wedding night – and plays with it, mocking all traditional attitudes and platitudes about marriage. There is much of the wild physical action that marks his other plays; as he himself says in his (fairly extensive) stage directions, "the over-the-top extremity of this physical world, should establish the kind of physical piece this is."

The physicality of the play is one of the first breaks with the Greek original. Standing so close to the origins of Greek drama, Aeschylus' play is one of his most static. It is a play of song and dance, and while both are very much present in Mee's (re)make, in Aeschylus' day the dance, in particular, would have been very formal. From what we know of ancient choral dance, there was little individual expression; the twelve men of the chorus would have moved in unison in steps prescribed by Aeschylus' orchestration in the matching turns of the *strophe* and *antistrophe* by which the choral actors moved around the *orchestra*, the dancing floor.

The story of the Danaids and their dreadful marriage is unusual. In its basic outline it is an aetiological myth, explaining the origins of the people of Argos in a way that allows them to trace their ancestry back to Zeus. It may also underlie latent hostility between those who lived in the Peloponnesus of Greece and those who resided in Egypt and along the North African coast. An ancestral Zeus is based on the myth of Io. According to the story, Zeus found Io, princess of Argos and priestess of Hera, attractive and as usual swept down to make love to her, drawing her into the nearby woods, and covering the grove with clouds. From Mt. Olympus Hera saw the clouds and was at once suspicious; upon her approach Zeus quickly turned Io into a white cow. (104) Hera demanded the cow as a gift, then set a guard to watch her, and after the guard was killed, sent a gadfly to haunt her. In torment Io fled from Argos, east across the water dividing Europe and Asia, thus giving that channel its name, Bosporus ("cow-crossing"). At last she arrived in Egypt, where Zeus restored her form and, in time, she gave birth to Epaphus, from whose son the Egyptians traced their ancestry. This, then, is the background to the Danaid story: the descendants of Epaphus could, through several generations, trace their lineage back to Argos and hence to Zeus. From this legend Aeschylus composed his trilogy, in which *Suppliant Maidens* stands first.

In the ensuing mythic years from the time of Io and Epaphus, brothers fought over lands along the North African coast. When the brother of Danaus offered his fifty sons to marry Danaus' fifty daughters, Danaus ignored the offer and fled with his maidens to Argos. But the

Egyptian suitors hotly pursued him. It is this point in the myth that Aeschylus presents in his *Suppliant Maidens*. He shows how Danaus asked Pelasgus for asylum, and that the Argive king agreed when the daughters threatened to hang themselves on the city altars.(105) Soon the suitors arrive, a mock marriage is staged, and all but one of the brides, per agreement with their father, kill their husbands on their wedding night. Hypermnestra spared her mate, was brought to trial, but, through the intervention of Aphrodite, she was acquitted.(106) With her husband she became the progenitor of the great heroes of Argos.

For *Big Love* Mee turned to this story of forced marriage and revenge, taking for his scaffold Aeschylus' extant play, and adding bits of information from the wider myth as well, and, of course and as usual, scraps of contemporary culture about marriage from those who believe in it and those who do not.(107) Mee had seen a production of *Les Danaides* by the Romanian director, Silviu Purcarete, at a stone quarry near Avignon in 1996, a play which started from Aeschylus' drama for Act I and invented action for a second act (108) and the experience influenced Mee to consider the Greek original.

His (re)making is a far more interesting play than that seen by the Athenians in 470 BC; indeed, as noted above, it is one of Mee's most often performed dramas. While closely following in structure Aeschylus' play – more closely than the *Bacchae 2.1* to its original and far more so than *True Love* to Euripides' *Hippolytus* – *Big Love* bounds joyously beyond the static choral drama from which Mee started.

Here, too, we find that Mee has kept that choral aspect of the earlier play in which there is far more song than dialogue. In *Big Love* Mee has included the entire repertoire of popular wedding music. At various points in the play we hear Pachelbel's *Canon in D*, the "Wedding March" from Mozart's *Marriage of Figaro*, Wagner's "Wedding March" from *Lohengrin*, Handel's "Arrival of the Queen of Sheba" from *Solomon* and Mendelssohn's "Wedding March" from *Midsummer Night's Dream*. In addition to the wedding music, Mee has included other songs that are as usual completely appropriate for his theme. Shortly after their entrance the brides offer a stirring rendition of Leslie Gore's *You Don't*

Own Me, words which underscore their position exactly: their ardent pursuers think that they have the right to marry them because of a long-ago contract. In the modern western world, the union of a man and a woman cannot be based on a piece of paper signed without the input of both parties. In this battle of the sexes, Mee also wants trumpet music to be heard. But he does not select strident martial pieces, but asks that we hear the more dulcet notes of Stanley's *Trumpet Tune*, or Clarke's *Trumpet Voluntary*, the latter a piece (oddly) almost always played on the organ. Finally, Giuliano, hopelessly in way over his head in the controversy that has arrived on his doorstep, at one point sings, "*Bewitched, Bothered and Bewildered am I.*"

Big Love is set in a seaside villa in Italy, a place to which the Danaid sisters have fled from Greece and their Greek-American would-be suitors. These women are seeking refuge in a foreign land, as did the original Danaids, but they claim that they are, in fact, related to the residents of the villa:

LYDIA   [thinking quickly]
   Oh. But.
   We are related.
   I mean, you know: in some way.
   Our people came from Greece to Sicily a long time ago
   and to Siracusa
   and from Siracusa to Taormina and to the Golfo di Saint'
Eufemia
   and from there up the coast of Italy to where we are now.
   So we are probably members of the same family you and I.
PIERO [amused]
   Descended from Zeus, you mean.
OLYMPIA
   Yes. We're all sort of goddesses in a way.
PIERO
   Indeed. It's very enticing to recover a family connection to
Zeus.

The lines are vintage Mee: transposing the ancient story to a very plausible modern argument. And while we can certainly laugh at the idea, it is not, after all, so very different from those today who seek to find ancestral connections to important figures through complex genealogy.

At first the fleeing brides seem to think the villa, into which they bring all their luggage — and later their wedding gifts — is a fancy hotel. After the owners have explained that it is a home, not a hotel, the women argue that they should be allowed to stay — not only are they related, as per the passage cited above, but that the Italian hosts should offer them refuge and asylum. When Piero (the up-dated Pelasgus) demurs, they, as their Greek counterparts, threaten to hang themselves, here from the villa porches, not the city altars.

In this play Mee has removed any direct characterization of the deities — nor does a god enter in Aeschylus' *Suppliant Maidens* until the final *deus ex machina* — but he does bring in a deity in disguise. This is Bella, the aged mother of Piero and Giuliano and ten other sons. Early in the play she enters the villa courtyard with a basket of ripe tomatoes to sort for sale. As she describes each of her sons, she picks up a tomato; if she finds one in some way wanting, she splats the tomato on the ground; she sets aside and saves a tomato for each son she favors. The scene is, at the time, amusing, although somewhat disconcerting: a son can be discarded as carelessly as an overripe tomato. It is only at the final portion of the play that we come to realize Bella is a stand-in for a Greek divinity and, here, probably for Aphrodite. Bella had dismissed her sons as carelessly as the ancient goddess discarded mortals who in some way displeased her. Aphrodite destroyed Hippolytus through Phaedra, for example, and, it should be noted, even Artemis whom Hippolytus exclusively worshipped left him without a tear as he lay dying. At the end of *Big Love*, when Lydia is put on trial by her sisters for falling in love with her spouse Nikos, Bella speaks up in favor of love and marriage. Her words are very similar to those the love goddess speaks, *ex machina*, at the end of the Danaid trilogy, a speech preserved only in fragments and the only part of the last play extant.

Hardly has Piero agreed to consider the brides as house guests when the fast-talking Greek American suitors arrive by helicopter. They seem more intent on honoring the contract by which they got the brides than acknowledging that they are in love with the women. It is clear, indeed, that they hardly know their would-be brides, but they do know they are supposed to have them. They have not heard Thyona sing *You Don't Own Me* and would not understand it if they had.

Constantine's argument on his rights is cut short by Piero's entrance and, being the gracious host, he invites the suitors in for drinks, cigars, and a rational discussion. At this point the male position is that such conflicts can be resolved without emotion or violence; they understand their rights and see no reason to humor the emotions of the would-be brides. To complete and emphasize the role-reversal here, Thyona bursts into a speech of rage, during which she begins to throw herself violently again and again on the floor. She punctuates her physical tantrum by shouting again and again that she does "not need a man," adding line after line of denigrating and desecrating descriptions of the male sex. Her sisters watch her tantrum and then Olympia joins in, so that each woman is throwing herself down, getting up, repeating the action in a "choreographed piece;" Mee directs that music should begin to accompany them, suggesting Bach's "Sleepers Awake" from *Cantata* No. 140, a piece that can only provide a peaceful contrast to the violence of the women's action. Finally Lydia joins in, but with her entrance into the wild action the women's thoughts turn to what they want in a man, opening their catalog with a reversal of Henry Higgins' famous song from Lerner and Lowe's *My Fair Lady*:

All Three Women Together
  Why can't a man
  be more like a woman?

Thyona, Olympia and Lydia close the scene with the quiet summation that if men and women can be together in harmony, all might know "what it is to live life on earth."

114

This is a comedy, of course, and Giuliano entering with wagons and carts of wedding gifts, returns the play to its comic mode. For he asks if he might keep the beautiful white satin ribbons from the gift boxes for his collection of Barbies and Kens, dolls whom he then describes in some detail. The following scenes shift the focus again, this time to the gifts themselves.

Olympia finds some of the gifts attractive and begins to consider the possibilities of a honeymoon; her resolve to hate men is clearly fading before the option of acquiring nice things and having a nice life. Her sisters counter her suggestions, but the entry of the real houseguests, Eleanor and Leo, with more wedding presents and words describing the joys of love, further weaken Olympia's resolve and even Lydia begins to find the two guests and their suggestions attractive. Indeed, Leo and Lydia dance "a long long, slow, intimate, father-daughter dance" to the music of Handel's "Air" from *Water Music Suite No. 1*. It is with such music and dance that Mee connects his (re)made play with its ancient origins. At the close of the dance, the play suddenly becomes a love story: both Thyona and Olympia, before dashing off admit they would like love, and Nikos joins Lydia on stage. These are the modern Hypermnestra and Lycurgus, these are the two who will find big love.

Mee is on his own here, for the extant text of *Suppliant Maidens* does not show the couple meeting. The modern play, of course, demands that the two develop a relationship that will encourage Lydia to break her promise to her father and sisters, to stand up for the possibility of love and happiness. In the ancient play Hypermnestra will be violating a (new) civil law and thus the intervention of Aphrodite is necessary to support her decision. Indeed the goddess' argument (as much as it can be determined from the fragment we have) is rather similar to that Apollo will make in the final play of the *Oresteia* trilogy, which Aeschylus wrote some 20 years later. There the god who has urged Orestes to his matricide and supports his deed argues that the love of a man and a woman, husband and wife, must be considered and honored as it reflects the marriage of Zeus and Hera (*Eum.* 213-220). In *Big Love* Mee does not explicitly argue for the sanctity of marriage and no law, civil or otherwise, is part of the script. But, in the end, Lydia's choice to spare her husband is the act to which the play is directed.

In their initial (on stage) meeting, Nikos does all the talking, leaving Lydia only to echo his final words. She understands what he is saying, however, and continues to find him attractive. Finally given a chance to speak, Lydia tells him her long and complicated dream. Dreams were important in ancient Greek culture. Dream therapy was the method of cure practiced at the sanctuaries of Asklepios, the healing god, and Hippocrates also considered dreams a clue to medical ailments. God-sent dreams are part of the epic stories told by Homer in his *Iliad* and *Odyssey*.(109) There are significant dreams in several extent tragedies as well. In Aeschylus' *Libation Bearers*, Clytemnestra's dream of birthing and nursing a serpent inspires her to send (at last) offerings to Agamemnon's tomb (*LB:* 523-541), Hecuba dreams of her son's death in the opening scene of her play (*Hec:* 68-89) and Iphigeneia's dream in the *Iphigeneia at Tauris* (*IT:* 42-62) leads her to change her usual course of action, a change which sets up the play's dramatic tension.

In *Big Love* Nikos easily interprets Lydia's dream: the unexpected happens. Like love. Music brings the truth of their situation to conclusion; here Mee designates "the heartbreaking music of the "Largo" from Bach's *Air on the G-String,* during which Nikos leads Lydia in a long slow and sweet dance. The two kiss and then Lydia runs off, realizing what she has done. Nikos, too, realizes what has happened and begins to swear and throw himself to the ground as the women had done earlier.

Soon his brothers enter and join in his physical expression of his rage and despair. Mee directs that during this male version of the throwing-to-the-ground violence Marc-Antoine Charpentier's *Prelude to Te Deum* be played at full volume, sound that almost drowns out the men's shouted words. These words themselves are not so important, but the suitors' emotion and "over the top" physicality is. For the suitors have discovered that the masculinity they have been taught to seek and for which they are expected to seek approval is not helpful in the present situation and they do not know how to react. Indeed, total madness and chaos erupts on stage, as the men rip off their shirts, throw things, and then fall upon each other.

As their tantrum ends, Constantine begins quietly to explain how difficult it is to be a man, an explanation that shifts to how war destroys a man, especially when he is expected to be re-integrated into society. Mee's familiar anti-war sentiments surface here, right on target for the time in which he wrote *Big Love*. While the play is a critique of marriage and its implications, it is, here at least, a vehicle for Mee to descry war once again. Constantine sets out clearly how difficult it is for a man who has been trained to kill to treat anyone gently, especially the woman in his bed .(110) His long monologue closes with words that echo those Eleanor spoke earlier, but as an ending to a speech on war and violence, the words have a stronger impact:

> . . . because to know this pain
> is to know the whole of life
> before we die
> and not just some pretty piece of it
> to know who we are
> both of us together
> this is a gift that a man can give a woman.

After the violence, after the chaos, *Big Love* suddenly becomes a play about marriage once again, and it appears that the weddings will take place as per the suitors' wishes. It is a wonderful charade. Indeed, the audience can begin to believe that everyone has taken Lydia's point of view, that marriage is a viable option. Eleanor enters with a huge wedding cake and Olympia asks that it have candles. But, of course, it is but a charade, although only the women know this. Piero and his brothers, as well as the houseguests Eleanor and Leo, believe that a wedding will take place, Piero in particular believing that he has found a way to make accommodation for the situation. Indeed, first Olympia and then Lydia are willing to consider the option; it is only Thyona who continues to argue that there will be no wedding that day.

But Thyona is apparently wrong. Piero is sorry, but he cannot take the risk of protecting them. He has made his accommodation, which is to agree with the suitors:

Your cousins will marry you
whether you want to marry them or not.
None of you has a choice.

The women hear his words in silence; Lydia and Olympia are ready to give in to their situation. But Thyona will not allow it. We have to take care of ourselves, she argues, we have to kill our husbands on our wedding night, because all men understand is force. Her sisters reject her plan – they cannot kill their husbands! Their fate has been determined by the myth, however, and they must, finally, agree. But they must also go through with the wedding, and once again the play veers to the present, as Olympia frets she does not have the Monique Lhuillier wedding gown she always dreamed of, not even a Vera Wang. Eleanor helps her and her sisters into their gowns, assuring them their wedding will be beautiful.

As they dress to kill, beautiful music underlines their actions: it is still a wonderful charade. The three suitors, plus 47 others march in dressed in formal attire; the three brides, with 47 others, beautifully decked out take their places while Wagner's "Wedding March" from *Lohengrin* plays out at full volume. The wedding takes place! Eleanor cuts the cake and the brides feed a piece to their grooms — although Thyona smashes hers into Constantine's face.

The two begin to dance and then to fight by dance as Handel's "Arrival of the Queen of Sheba" from *Solomon* fills the stage. The other brides and suitors also begin a riot of violence accompanied now by the thundering wild, violent, Dionysian music of Widor's "Toccata" from *Organ Symphony No 5*.(111) This chaotic group action scene is Mee's updating of the choral dance and song of his original, brought to the modern stage to express the anger and anguish of the myth Aeschylus had chosen to present.(112)

And then the mythic action is fulfilled, and each bride in her own way kills her husband. Except for one: during the chaos and the killings, Lydia and Nikos are off on the side alone, making love.

A quiet descends upon the scene. Piero and Giuliano enter, and step stunned amidst the carnage, while Bella chastises him for not stopping this. Suddenly Thyona realizes Lydia is with Nikos, whom she introduces as her husband. At once Thyona turns upon her sister in disbelieving anger. Piero stops her rage and suggests a trial, and Bella steps forth as judge.

Lydia's defense is simple: she does not want to live in a world where love is not possible. Thyona counters her with an irrational tirade about justice and its failure and what happens to a world in which justice is ignored. Olympia, meanwhile, offers the typical excuse: I was just following orders. It is Bella who speaks out on Lydia's behalf and on the power and importance of love.

Many might not realize this final scene of Mee's play is, in fact, a direct echo of several of the dramas seen in the Theater of Dionysus in Athens. The Greek forerunners of the trial scene on stage include the trial of Helen in Euripides' *Trojan Women*, and that of Polymestor in his *Hecuba*, while the Athenian's love of the jury-trial is wonderfully parodied by Aristophanes in his *Wasps*.(113) The most famous trial scene in drama, one could well argue, is that of the Furies versus Orestes in the final play of Aeschylus' *Oresteia*, the *Eumenides*, a play said to recall the original establishment of the trial by jury. In that text Athena claims the matter is too serious to be decided by a single vote and sets up the jury court, a creation which may be Athens' greatest gift to modern civilized society. There seems to have been a trial at the end of the Danaid trilogy as well. But there the final decision was (apparently) made by Aphrodite, who appears *deus ex machina* at the end of the play. Here it is Bella who takes on the role of the goddess. As noted above, Bella was introduced as someone who stands apart and who makes fateful decisions in the manner of a Greek deity. Here she defends Lydia's choice, asserting that "love is the highest law."

Having made her decision and asserted that life is beautiful when touched by love, Bella first, then Giuliano, catalogue all the wonders which make up the modern world. Mee, as I noted previously, is fond of the catalogue, offering in each play a long listing of various objects and numerous ideas. This catalogue is a mixed collage from many parts of nature and human life. As their words stop Mendelssohn's "Wedding March" from *Midsummer Night's Dream* begins and returns the play to its major theme.

Lydia and Nikos begin to make their way along a quickly formed receiving line, with Nikos stopping for a brief exchange on life and love with Piero. The loud music prevents the audience from hearing their words, although Mee offers extensive suggestions as to what they might be saying. The unheard dialogue is a further example of how Mee prefers action to speech, proving that action literally speaks louder than words. For Mee, the stage picture is more important than the verbal exchange.

At the end of the receiving line all stop for a family photo. Lydia tosses her bouquet into the audience and then she and Nikos exit up the center aisle. They no longer look like the happy couple; in fact, Mee writes, "they both look shell-shocked and devastated." They have taken the first step to love and, perhaps, happiness, but at what cost; more importantly, who can predict today that a marriage will fulfill the couples' dreams and desires.

Big Love is both a play about love and a critique of the institution of marriage. Mee took the strange story of the Danaids and played it out both ways: literally, for the brides, all but one, did murder their husbands, and figuratively through the many lines about the nature of men and women, of marriage and of the power of love. As his "tragedies" have much comedy in them, so his "comedy" has a serious message. Both men and women have to respect each other and the institutions of their society. Love is something Big, but it is difficult to find. Nevertheless, the quest must be made for the prize is worth fighting for and is worth finding.

CHAPTER VI

(Re) Making Tragedy

In the plays I have discussed in these pages, Charles Mee has recreated the ancient dramas in a way relevant to the contemporary world. The issues that the ancient dramatists presented as part of the world in which they lived are also those faced by people in the late twentieth and early twenty-first centuries.

In the plays of his trilogy *Imperial Dreams,* based on the House of Atreus legend, *Orestes 2.0, Agamemnon 2.0,* and *Iphigeneia 2.0,* Mee uses the myth to speak out against the vanity and horror of war. As a long-time pacifist the playwright culled the web for blogs and other texts written by those who had experienced the suffering of military conflicts. The dramas of Aeschylus, Sophocles, and Euripides frequently spoke out against war and Mee's plays follow this tradition. In these three plays the myths remain virtually unchanged, the lines are often repeated verbatim from old text to new and the ideas presented on the Athenian stage are expressed in Mee's various dramatic spaces. He, like the ancient dramatists, speaks out against the violence and madness of war, the ruin resulting from lust misplaced, the suffering men and women cause to each other, often deliberately but more frequently by random chance.

These (re)made Greek plays are complex scripts. On the recreating of ancient plays for the modern stage Mee himself has written:

> One of the great pleasures in a work of art that knows it comes from the culture is that, inevitably, inherently, it contains a tension between the past and the present, the given and the possible, the enduring and the ephemeral.(114)

The tension he describes here is what makes the (re)made plays so exciting. We see the old stories, the old framework, or "scaffolding" as he calls it, but on that frame we also see many aspects of the world around us. Some of these we recognize and accept; others we recognize and realize we have deliberately chosen to ignore. Through his characters Mee does not allow us that choice: the culture around us is comprised of all its parts, those we admire, those we abhor. Mee's frequent catalogues in their wide-ranging completeness catch our attention because they startle as well as please.

Often Mee's jarring juxtapositions seem to force his creations to crash away from the works of the ancient dramatists. I argue, however, that despite the explicit and often ugly language, despite the boisterous action and often cacophonous diction, Mee has written tragedies for the modern world. When Agamemnon returns to the stage with the body of his daughter in the closing scene of *Iphigeneia 2.0*, his entrance halts the action on stage and brings the audience to tears as it compels them to understand the full sense of the tragedy which the choice for war has initiated.

The three Greek-based plays that Mee terms "Tragedies" direct audience attention to other themes. *Bacchae 2.1* celebrates Dionysus, god of nature in all its sexuality and the way in which his cult must be practiced. While his play gives us lines of heart-breaking beauty when focused on the deity's role as nature-god, it remains a cautionary tale. Mee's play follows the lead of its original by showing what happens when a political leader tries to stop the religious desires of his citizens; it also reflects Euripides' warning against excess. In his script Mee expands the two themes until we recognize that these issues are still with us and still bring disaster upon those who do not recognize the dangers they present.

The next two plays of the "Tragedy" series focus on the many varieties and possibilities of love. Here Mee has moved further away from his sources and allowed his stories to play out beyond their ancient framework. By uniting *Trojan Women* with the fourth book of Vergil's *Aeneid*, Mee reveals Aphrodite's hand behind the suffering experienced by the characters of both stories. His *Trojan Women – A Love Story* is closely linked to that of Euripides; to make his anti-war message Mee did not have to alter very much of what the Greek dramatist had written. In the second part of his drama, however, Mee expanded his original to show how the Trojan War had consequences beyond its time and place. As he discussed in *Playing God*, men frequently fail to understand how events are connected or recognize "the rule of unintended consequences."(115)

True Love puts on stage characters who discuss, from their own experience, all possible examples of love and lust. Mee admits that this third play in the tragedy series is just this side of pure "riff," and we might well wonder if it has a message for its audience. In *True Love*, despite its title, much of the love is destructive and for the garage residents love is more a source of pain than pleasure. For although Plato's *Symposium* lies behind the script, there is no vision of Perfect Love in Mee's text. At the close of *True Love*, it is the ruin seen in Euripides' *Hippolytus* that marks Mee's play. The playwright's message for the modern audience suggests that our quest for happiness via love has, at best, an ambiguous outcome.

The ambiguity of happy love repeats in *Big Love*, the comedy (re) made from a tragedy, the comedy based on a bizarre and bloody myth. The boisterous physicality of the play seems to mock the idea of love and marriage; in the end, however, love wins out against all odds. In his dramatic analysis of love and marriage, Mee suggests that men and women can respect both the institutions of their society and each other, but that to do so is not easy. While, as Bella says, "Love trumps all," her words can only ring true if respect also stands firm. A tragedy may be made into a comedy, but comedy can slip into tragedy unless one is very very careful.

In his (re)making project Charles Mee recreates the plots set out in the ancient Greek texts in plays that resonate in our own times. The issues that the ancient dramatists presented as part of the world in which they lived are those faced by people in current times. But men and women today meet these issues in a world that is not clean, clear-cut, or directed by gods. We live in a world shattered by such realities and distractions as Mee describes. While keeping much of the original script, the playwright transforms Greek tragedy into something new. In the final scenes of Euripides' plays the audience sees men or women ruined through the designs of the divinities. The Greek characters stepped forth boldly to achieve their goals, only to realize that by their actions they have fulfilled the plans of the gods. Charles Mee shows men and women who also come to ruin, but there are no deities guiding their choices. His characters step forth in a world over which they seem to have little control, but it is a world, nevertheless, that they have created. And the reality they find is harsh and very much present. Mee's characters rebel, they struggle, they engage in violent physical activity and speak out in catalogues of what they know, like and desire. But in the end, ruin falls upon them as it did their Greek originals. We as audience can find no solace for them or for ourselves by turning to any god.

Despite the close connections in characters, words, and themes, Charles Mee's plays are entirely new creations: he has (re)made the ancient plays into scripts for the modern stage, showing his audience a world that is at times strange and, at other times, frighteningly familiar. The oft-spoken line of many characters, "It's a nightmare, really" defines the dramas that Mee has composed for today's audiences. These dramas, I argue here, offer a new form of tragedy. This new form may be more appropriate for the modern world than that offered by Aristotle or the ancient playwrights. Each man and woman must find a way to create – or (re)create – a meaning that responds to a world of which they have but a small part in defining. The modern world is shaped more by its prevalent culture than by deities such as those in whom the ancients believed.

In the dramas I have discussed here Mee has rewritten the ancient myths in a way appropriate for today. His tragic vision is not that of the

Greek originals, but through his scripts he suggests that for the current world (that of the last years of the twentieth century and first years of the twenty-first) the ancient themes can help define a new form of tragedy. Through his (re)making project Mee has transformed tragedy. The (re) made tragedy is not tied to the universal but to the individual. The jagged pieces of the modern world have cut away the great overarching ideals. The contemporary dramatist who wants to write tragedies appropriate for today must present on stage plays that show the pain, agony, and suffering of the individual in a world he or she has created, either by deliberate choice or random chance. Charles Mee's plays show us this world.

End Notes

For INTRODUCTION: *pp. 1-7*

1. Scott Cummings, *Remaking American Theater. Charles Mee, Anne Bogart, and the SITI Company* (Cambridge, 2006): 60. Mee's description of his work is cited by most authors who write about him; he himself does so in every interview.

2. Cummings, *Remaking*: 5. Cummings writes, "Some of Mee's plays… have no single, discernible antecedent, but there is always some aspect of the work that is building on the past."

3. Charles Mee, "Shaped in bits, drips and quips" in "Playwrights on Writing" *LA Times*, October 24, 2004.

For BIOGRAPHY: *pp. 9-16*

4. Charles Mee, *A Nearly Normal Life* (Boston, 1999). In his book Mee documents not only his own story but also a history of the way doctors tried to find cures for the disease, many of which were very painful and mostly unsuccessful. As his book tells his story so well, I will only include some brief points here.

5. Mee, *A Nearly Normal Life*: 40-41.

6. Mee, *Life*: 21.

7. Mee, *Life*: 33.

8. Mee, *Life*: 182-83.

9. Mee, *Life*. 184.

10. Scott Cummings, *Remaking American Theater. Charles Mee, Anne Bogart, and the SITI Company* (Cambridge, 2006): 17.

11. Mee's history books include *The End of Order: Versailles 1919* (1980), *The Marshall Plan: The Launching of Pax Americana* (1987), and *The Genius of the People* (1987), a discussion of the 1787 Constitutional Convention.

12. Cited from interview with Joseph Mandell, "Falling In, Falling Out: Love's Cycle Of Rebirth," *New York Times* (Arts / Theater) September 02, 2001: 5.

13. Cummings, *Remaking*. 22.

14. Cummings, *Remaking*. 28-31, discusses the play, terming it a "satyr play" to the trilogy that precedes it.

15. Erin B. Mee, "Shattered and Fucked Up and Full of Wreckage: The Words and Works of Charles L. Mee," *Tulane Drama Review* 46 no3 83 (Fall 2002): 87

16. Cited from my interview with Charles Mee, November 6, 2010. The information may also be found in Robert A. Schanke, editor, *Angels in the American Theater: Patrons, Patronage, and Philanthropy*. (Carbondale, 2007): 89, a relationship Schanke identifies as one "without parallel or precedent in American theatrical philanthropy."

17. Mee's honors include (among others) a Lifetime Achievement award in drama from the American Academy of Arts and Letters, two OBIE Awards, for *Vienna: Lusthaus* (1986) and *Big Love* (2002)), and the Fisher Award given by the Brooklyn Academy of Music.

For ANCIENT ATHENIAN DRAMA: *pp. 17-21*

18. The tripods were displayed on high along the street winding around the east of the Acropolis to the theater; to this day that street is called Tripod Street, although the bronze trophies have long since disappeared.

19. Only two instances are known when a playwright tried to present an actual historical event on stage. Phrynichus, one of the earliest writers of tragedy, presented a play titled the *Capture of Miletus*, which caused such distress in the audience that he was fined and historical subject matter was banned. But some twenty years later Aeschylus did so successfully in his *Persians*, and scholars today debate how he managed to show his Athenian audience their conquest of Xerxes in a way that allowed them to accept the story and feel at least some sympathy for the vanquished ruler.

20. At the close of the Sicilian Expedition (Athens' ill-fated attempt to invade Sicily during the Peloponnesian War in the years 415-13 BC), the defeated Athenians were held in the stone quarries of Sicily (Thuc. VII.86-87). Some prisoners, according to Plutarch (*Nicias* 29), were given better treatment when they sang choral passages from Euripides: "Several were saved for the sake of Euripides, whose poetry, it appears, was in request among the Sicilians more than among any of the settlers out of Greece."

21. Some thirty-three tragedies and eleven comedies survive from the many hundreds that were written in ancient Athens. A full history of the development of Greek drama is available in many books and numerous websites; a very good history can be found in P.E. Easterling *The Cambridge Companion to Greek Tragedy* (Cambridge, 1997) or a good discussion in P.E. Easterling and Bernard M.W. Knox (eds.): *The Cambridge History of Classical Literature* (Cambridge, 1989).

For ANCIENT GREEK DRAMA RETOLD: *pp. 23-28*

22. Peter Holland, "Space: the Final Frontier" in H. Scolnicov and P. Holland, *The Play Out of Context* (Cambridge, 1989): 47.

23. The origin of Greek drama, of course, lies in the chorus. But it would not be unusual for there to be a group of citizens before the royal palace or gathered in the town's marketplace; such a group is out of place in the living or bedroom (as shown, for example, in T. S. Eliot's *Family Reunion*). It is only in his *Orestes* that Euripides suggests the chorus is an unwelcome visitor to the palace of Electra and her brother.

24. Marianne McDonald, *Ancient Sun, Modern Light* (Columbia UP, 1992): 5. In my pages, this quotation relates to the plays of Charles Mee, a playwright not discussed in her book.

25. Gershon Shaked, "The Play: Gateway to Cultural Dialogue," in Scolnicov and Holland, *The Play Out of Context*: 13.

26. David Johnston, "Building Bridges," Program notes for the production of his translation of *Dog in the Manger* at the American Shakespeare Theatre (Washington, DC) in February-March, 2009.

27. I write tragedy here, not comedy, because the ancient comedians created their own plots tied to the political and social concerns of Athens of the 5th century. Tragedians, on the other hand, based dramas on ancient myth. Aeschylus' *Persians* is the only play derived from an historical event (see above n. 2).

28. James Redmond puts forth the idea that "it is the irrelevant plays that do not lose their savour with the years." See James Redmond, "If the salt have lost his savour": some 'useful' plays in and out of context on the London Stage" in Scolnicov and Holland, *The Play Out of Context*: 63-88; my quotation comes from Scolnicov's introduction p. 3.

For THE *IMPERIAL DREAMS* TRILOGY: *ORESTES 2.0: pp. 29-45*
29. The plays of the "Theban Trilogy" are *Oedipus Tyrannus, Oedipus at Colonus,* and *Antigone.* Sophocles wrote the *Antigone* in 442 BC, *Oedipus Tyrannus* in 428 BC and the *Colonus* was his last play, written in 406 BC and produced after his death in 401 BC.

30. See, among others, Anne Burnett, *Catastrophe Survived* (Oxford, 1971): 183-212; she argues (184) that the subject of the play is failure.

31. Mee told his story to me during our discussion on October 6, 2010.

32. See Karelisa Hartigan, *Ambiguity and Self-Deception* (Lang, 1991): 127-156.

33. Charles Mee, "Shaped in Bits, Drips and Quips," in LA Times Series, Playwrights on Writing (October 24, 2004): 2

34. Elaine Scarry, *The Body in Pain* (Oxford, 1985): 123. Indeed, all the interjections made by Tapemouth Man repeat passages from Scarry's important work.

35. Philoctetes, wounded by a sacred serpent when he inadvertently steps into holy ground, was isolated from his troops on a deserted island when the Greek soldiers found his screams of pain too disturbing. The relevance of his story to contemporary war has been explored by Bryan Doerries in his Theater of War project during the early years of the twenty-first century.

36. Again Tapemouth's words reflect Scarry's discussion in *The Body in Pain:* 108-111.

37. So Mee said in my interview with him [October 6, 2010].

38. For example, in the *Iphigeneia at Tauris* Euripides deliberately blocks the escape plan so that Athena can arrive; the appearance of the Dioscouroi at the end of his *Electra* is hardly necessary, and in his *Philoctetes* Sophocles so crafts the action that Heracles must come to resolve the conflict.

39. Among others, see Norman Austin, Helen *of Troy and her Shameless Phantom* (Cornell University Press: 1994) and Karelisa Hartigan, "Helen so Fatefully Named: The Continuity of her Myth in Modern Greek Poetry." *Classical and Modern Literature* 4 (1983): 17-24.

For *AGAMEMNON 2.0:* pp. 48-56
40. David Schweizer directed *Orestes 2.0*, Oskar Eustis, *Electra*.

41. Atreus' violent deed was his vengeance on Thyestes for the latter's seduction of his wife and attempt to usurp his throne. Crimes and vengeance mark the family's history from its origins on Mt. Olympus to the final exile of Agamemnon's son Orestes. No house of ancient myth is filled with so many violent deeds; no house is the subject of so many tragedies, both ancient and modern.

42. Reported by Steven Leigh Morris, "Greek Love: Charles L. Mee's *Agamemnon,* and Sarah Ruhl's *Demeter in the City*" in *LA Weekly* (June 22, 2006): 1.

43. The *Agamemnon 2.0,* as the *Orestes 2.0,* reflects Elaine Scarry's arguments. Her discussion of the soldier's declaration that he is going "to die for his country," or "to kill for his country" is a masterful description of how these few words lay aside all common ideas of how the body should be treated; see pp. 121 – 124: "Referential Instability."

44. Mee culled these reports from the internet blogs; within a few years they were no longer allowed to be posted (a detail confirmed by Mee in my interview with him October 6, 2010). In 2010 the Wikileaks

information broke into the news, and America learned of violence such as that reported in the earlier blogs.

45. For the cover of his translation of the *Oresteia*, Peter Meineck (Hackett, 1998) chose the 21 April 1951 photo of General MacArthur's tickertape parade in New York City, an event titled the "Welcome of Welcomes." Thus Meineck chose to close the gap between past and present through his cover illustration.

46. Homer's *Iliad*, of course, is filled with similes that describe the soldier's actions in terms of various beasts of prey. But it is the Bard who so adds these descriptive similes; no character ever so describes himself as an animal. For a discussion of Homer's animal similes, see my article, "He Rose Like a Lion: Animal Similes in Homer and Vergil." *Acta Antiqua* 21 (1973): 223-244.

47. The "Carpet Scene" is one of the few action-on-stage scenes in extant Greek tragedy. Most significant action scenes occur off stage and are reported by a messenger. Thus Aeschylus' innovation is doubly striking: the audience sees a man step forth to his doom.

48. Laura Hitchcock, Review of *Agamemnon* for *A CurtainUp Los Angeles Review* (July 7, 2006), posted on The Internet Theater Magazine of Reviews: www. curtainup.com.

For *IPHIGENEIA 2.0*: *pp. 57-70*
49. Aeschylus gives no reason for the deity's anger; Sophocles says he boasted he was a better hunter than Artemis (*El*: 568-70) and Euripides in *his Iphigeneia in Tauris* says her father forgot to fulfill for the goddess his vow to offer her the fairest thing the year bore to him (*IT* 19-24). But no cause for the deity's anger is given in this play; indeed no deity is present at all.

50. As noted above, Euripides had left Athens for Macedonia in 408 BC; he sent the *IA* for the Athenian City Dionysia just before his death in 406.

51. Mee requests "a male voice singing an ancient Macedonian folk song, wailing, almost keening. Or *Salpinx Call* by Nederlanders Blazers Ensemble with Bie Deti Dallget by Arap Celolesakaj, Fatbardha Brahimi, Nazif Celaj & Nikolin Likaj. Or the male solo from *Music of the Turkmen* from Primitive Music of the World. Or it could be Dionisis Savopoulos and Sotiria Bellou sing *Zeibekiko*. Or Nikos Xylouris sings the mournful *San Erthoun Mana I Fili Mou*. Or the very sad song *Ipne Pou Pernis Ta Pedia* sung by Savina Yannatou."

52. He suggests, indeed, "it might be the incredibly sprightly brass band from Yugoslavia Boban Markovic Orkestar performing *Disko— Dzummbus*, or the Macedonian brass band Maleshevski Melos performing *Nesatova Sa-Sa*." Mee has admitted that he often puts in ideas that appeal to him at any given moment, not that he expects this particular orchestra to come to his stage.

53. Charles Mee, *Playing God. Seven Fateful Moments When Great Men Met to Change the World* (Simon and Schuster, 1993).

54. Mee told me this during the October 6, 2010 interview; the information is also given by David Cote in his review of *Iphigeneia 2.0,* "Greek in Review Postmodern dramatist Charles Mee slices and dices ancient tragedy for today," posted at Time Out New York / Issue 619 : Aug 9–15, 2007

55. See Karelisa Hartigan, *Greek Drama on the American Stage: 1882-1994* (Greenwood, 1997): 15-19 *et passim.* Euripides wrote the play in 415 BC for the same reason: to call attention to the pain brought to the women whose men go to war.

56. See Scarry's full discussion, *The Body in Pain*: 121-124.

57. An exception to this flashback or recounting occurs in dramatic mysteries, most particularly, perhaps, in those of Agatha Christie.

58. Jonathan Shay, *Achilles in Vietnam. Combat Trauma and the Undoing of Character*. (Scribner, 1994).

59. Indeed, Euripides includes little of the familiar version of the story. The oracular command is given by a simple "if/then –if not/then not" formula (92-93): "There will be a sailing and a destruction of Troy if they sacrifice, if not, these things will not take place." Agamemnon must make the sacrifice only if he wants to make war on Troy.

For THREE TRAGEDIES - *THE BACCHAE 2.1: pp. 71-88*

60. Some reports claim Euripides was born in 484 BC, others, 480; the later date may reflect a desire to put his birth in the year of Athens' most important naval battle at Salamis. Ancient biographies tend to the bizarre: Sophocles was said to have choked on an olive pit (possible), Aeschylus killed when an eagle dropped a turtle on his head (unlikely).

61. This choral lyric contains (876-881/897-901) the lines often translated as "a thing of beauty is a joy forever." The Greek may be so translated, but the context is far different from Keats' ode, for the refrain's opening lines are "what is more beautiful than to hold your hand in victory over the head of your enemy whom you have just crashed."

62. The origins of Zeus himself were traced back to Crete, but myths tell that the births of Athena, Hermes, Apollo and Artemis occurred on the mainland or islands of Greece.

63. Barbara Ehrenreich, *Dancing in the Streets: A History of Collective Joy* (London, 2007): 39.

64. Others also comment upon the language of the attendants: "The juxtapositions are striking, creating word images of remarkable beauty and obscene discomfort.. . The plot becomes secondary to the exploration of language and the fullness of emotion," writes Dan Bacalzo in his review of the play (TheaterMania.com: March 28, 2001)

65. Mee's political leaders are not the first to speak in common and vulgar language. The Nixon tapes have revealed his penchant for swearing, and his successor was also known for his "colorful" Texan language.

66. There Prometheus offers a long list of his gifts that aid civilization (*PV*: 437-504), including such crafts as constructing homes and ships, such skills as agriculture and understanding nature's elements and divine omens, such abilities as using numbers and fighting disease: "all arts that mortals have come from Prometheus."

67. For a prurient Pentheus, see Charles Segal, *Interpreting Greek Tragedy* (Cornell, 1986) 283-292 and Froma Zeitlin, "Playing the Other: Theater, Theatricality, and the Feminine in Greek Drama" in *Nothing to Do with Dionysos?*, eds. J. Winkler and F. Zeitlin (Princeton, 1990): 63-74.

68. Many directors add serpents to the god's costume. One of the more memorable was that done in 1969 by the Yale School of Drama, where Dionysus holding a snake in his final epiphany, caught the attention of the play's reviewers; see Hartigan, *Greek Drama on the American Stage: 1882-1994*: 84.

69. In counter argument I could say that the on-stage redressing done by Butterfly in David Henry Hwang's play is spellbinding to watch. Here, however, I think Mee is going more for the prurient titillation than for the pity and fear the Greek version arouses.

70. During one interview Mee explained his collecting thus: "My plays are maybe half appropriated text and half stuff I write—because I didn't have time to find what I wanted. I think of those borrowed texts as historical documents, taken from the culture." Cited by David Cote in his review of *Iphigeneia 2.0*, "Greek in review: Postmodern dramatist Charles Mee slices and dices ancient tragedy for today," Internet review Time Out New York / Issue 619: Aug 9–15, 2007. Cote points out that the inserts are both shocking and profound.

71. For a discussion of the pastoral ideal in Mee's plays, see Elinor Fuchs (1994) "Play as Landscape: Another Version of Pastoral," *Theater* 25: 44-51. Her article is about his *Orestes*, but the words apply to this play as well.

72. In his masterful commentary on Euripides' *Bacchae*, E.R. Dodds (Oxford, 1960: at 1084-5) collects the ancient evidence for nature's traditional response to a divine epiphany.

73. Question and response from our discussion on October 6, 2010.

For *THE TROJAN WOMEN - A LOVE STORY:* pp. 89-98
74. Although Berlioz included the events of the fall of Troy in his script, only the last three acts were staged; Act III begins at Dido's palace at Carthage, Book IV of the *Aeneid*. Mee's script follows Berlioz's in location, although certainly not in presentation.

75. When Paris was born, Cassandra warned their mother Hecuba that her new son would bring destruction upon Troy and the baby was left on Mt. Ida. Having grown to manhood, he was approached to decide the beauty contest prompted by Eris and he judged Aphrodite the most beautiful. In time he returned and, against Cassandra's pleas, Paris was permitted to remain at the palace.

76. Palamedes was sent to Ithaca to recruit Odysseus to join the Greek expedition to Troy where he saw through the wily king's attempt to avoid the draft. Odysseus never forgave him, and at Troy set up a plot that made Palamedes look like a traitor; the Greeks, believing Odysseus' false letter, killed him. There was bitter irony in the plot, for legend says it was Palamedes who invented many letters of the Greek alphabet, so by using writing to destroy him Odysseus doubly turned the tables on his draft recruiter.

77. Thucydides reports the Melian incident in his *History* V.85-113.

78. Apollo had fallen in love with Cassandra and gave her the gift of prophecy. When she denied him in her bed, he did not take back his gift but cursed her by letting her tell the truth and never be believed. She had foreseen that Paris would bring ruin to Troy but no one listened; she now knows that the Greeks will suffer much on their return journey and that Agamemnon will not survive beyond his first evening home.

79. In addition to Irene Pappas as Helen, Cacoyannis' *Trojan Women* stars Katharine Hepburn as Hecuba, Vanessa Redgrave as Andromache and Geneviève Bujold as Cassandra. The script was closely based on Edith Hamilton's translation, the setting vast expanses of grit and stone (located mostly in north central Spain).

80. Cummings, *Remaking American Theater.* 68. He says the act is dubbed "The Musical" (although this is not on Mee's web-posted script); he quotes Michael Feingold as calling it "a ballad opera" in "War and Pieces," *Village Voice,* July 9, 1996: 67.

81. Cummings, *Remaking.* 68.

82. Fuchs, *Theater* 25: 48.

83. Mee wants his Dido to be different to show that this is another world into which Aeneas has sailed. One wonders, though, if the black

Carthaginian might recall to some audience members the misplaced theory put out by Martin Bernal in his controversial three-volume work, *Black Athena: The Afroasiatic Roots of Classical Civilization*, wherein Cleopatra is posited as being black. Cleopatra was Greek, Dido was Phoenician: neither was black. Mee sets up Dido's palace in Carthage as a spa: in reading the script I could not help imaging a scene such as that at Circe's palace in Andrei Konchalovsky's teleplay of the *Odyssey*.

84. Indeed, every scene of this act is marked by music and song. Mee includes over a dozen songs in his script; even he admits there are too many and suggests that some could be cut: "There are too many songs in this piece. I loved them all so much I couldn't cut any, but there are too many. Also, a director and actors may want to bring in other songs that they feel capture the essence of the piece. Feel free to do it." Each song is well-tied to the plot, but the play becomes too long if all are sung in full. This song, I argue, should not be cut.

85. Cummings, *Remaking*: 71.

86. The Second Punic War finally ended in the Roman's victory at Zama in 202 BC, when Scipio (hence forth called Africanus) defeated the clever Hannibal; the strategy of the battle has been studied by military historians ever since. The first Punic War (264-241) revealed to the Romans they needed a navy as well as an army; after the third (149-146) Rome plowed the land of Carthage with salt, leaving the people as desolate as were the Trojans after the Greeks burned their city to the ground.

87. As noted above in Introduction (5), Mee says that he leaves it up to his director and cast to choose which action they feel fits best with their understanding of the play.

88. Cummings, *Remaking*: 71-2.

For *TRUE LOVE* : *pp.99-108*

89. Mee, *A Nearly Normal Life*: 32-33. He realized he would have to exchange a life of physical activity to a life of the mind. "Henceforth, I would have to use my head. . . And so I filled it with Plato. In fact, I devoured the *Symposium* and asked Miss Strouss to bring me more."

90 Elyse Sommer, *True Love*. A *CurtainUp* Review, 26 November, 2001.

91. Euripides' earlier version of this story, *Hippolytus Veiled*, was fined for being indecent. He returned to the myth and offered the extant version for the 428 BC drama festival. For a full discussion of the earlier play, see Hanna Roisman, *Nothing Is As It Seems* (Lanham, MD, 1999): 1-26.

92. According to legend Theseus could claim two fathers: the King of Athens Aegeus who lay with the princess of Troizen, or Poseidon, whom the princess claimed was her son's true father. Theseus became king of Athens as being the son of Aegeus, while the sea god also answered his prayers – sometimes for good, at others for ill.

93. Cummings, *Remaking*: 76, so describes the cast of the play.

94. Quoted from Mee's introduction to his play in the collection *Divine Fire. Eight Contemporary Plays Inspired by the Greeks.* (Caridad Svich, ed.; New York, 2005): 212.

95. Racine's *Phèdre* reflects Euripides' play only tangentially; its complex plot hides the dangerous passions seen in the Greek version.

96. The gods are absent from Racine's drama as well. Although Mee lists the French play among his sources, he owes far less to it than to Euripides' drama.

97. The critical literature on the *Hippolytus* is vast. For this particular point, see esp. B. Knox, "The *Hippolytus* of Euripides," reprinted in *Word*

and Action (Johns Hopkins 1979): 205-230 and C.A.E. Luschnig, "Men and Gods in Euripides' *Hippolytus*," *Ramus* 9 (1980): 89-100.

98. In the fields around Trozina today, a particular type of bush is said to be the same as that behind which Phaedra hid, and that the markings on its leaves are where she stuck pins in her repressed desire. The ancient legends live on.

99. Cited from Sommer, *CurtainUp Review* (2001).

100. Mee saw the play in a quarry at the Avignon festival in 1996; several years later he wrote his version of Aeschylus' *Suppliants, Big Love*. Cited from Cummings, *Remaking:* 78; Mee confirmed the story in his interview with me on 6 October, 2010.

101. It is an odd recompense: neither Phaedra nor Hippolytus wanted their story told. But Greek deities have little understanding of mortal suffering, meanwhile using men and women for their own, often vengeful, purposes; here Artemis promises to harm someone Aphrodite loves (*Hipp.* 1420-22).

102. In Tauris Iphigeneia was to officiate at rites of human sacrifice. Again, the deities have no understanding of human suffering: the girl rescued from the altar was asked to stand over others caught in the same position she had been.

For TRAGEDY TO COMEDY: *BIG LOVE: pp. 109-120*
103. For many years scholars considered Aeschylus' *Suppliants* to be his first extant play and hence the first Greek tragedy. The Parian Marble/Chronicle, a chronological inscription found on the island of Paros in the 1600s, however, shows that the *Persians* was composed before the Danaid Trilogy, of which the *Suppliants* was the first tragedy, followed by the *Egyptians* and the *Daughters of Danaus*. Mee blends the events of all three plays.

104. There are alternate versions of the myth; this is the way Ovid told the story in his *Metamorphoses* I.583-750.

105. Again, there are various versions of the story; Aeschylus presented it thus it in his *Suppliants* and his version is reflected in Mee's (re)make of that play.

106. Aphrodite apparently arrives *deus-ex-machina* at the end of the final play; only fragments of her speech are extant, the play itself is not.

107. Mee's note at the end of the text lists these as Klaus Theweleit, Leo Buscaglia, Gerald G. Jampolsky, Valerie Solanus, Maureen Stanton, Lisa St Aubin de Teran, Sei Shonagon, Eleanor Clark, Barbara Grizzuti Harrison, Kate Simon, and Laurie Williams, among others. Several of these provided source material for his other plays as well.

108. See Steve Wilmer, "Improving Aeschylus. A Review of Les Danaides," *Didaskalia* III (1996/3), available on *Didaskali*a Home Page.

109. Hippocrates discusses dreams in his *Regimen IV*. God-sent dreams in the *Iliad* include that sent to Agamemnon by Zeus at *Iliad* II.5-36, and the one sent by Athena to Nausikaa in *Odyssey* VI 13-40. For dream therapy, see S. Oberhelmen, "The Diagnostic Dream in Ancient Medical Theory and Practice, *Bulletin of the History of Medicine* 61 (1987): 47-60 and K. Hartigan, *Performance and Cure* (Duckworth, 2008).

110. As in the tragedies, Mee is here drawing upon the work of Elaine Scarry, *The Body in Pain*. But Constantine's words could well be taken from any news report printed during the wars in Iraq and Afghanistan, wars which have left numerous men suffering from PSTD and unable to re-integrate into society, especially one that does not fully support the military conflict.

111. For the killings Mee notes that perhaps Widor's music is good for a cast of hundreds (!) but a smaller cast production might need more quiet music for the ritualized murders.

112. Mee offers paragraphs of suggested actions, violent, lewd, indeed quite mad things the various brides and grooms could be doing, adding that they do not have to be doing his suggestions exactly, but anything and everything that is over the top "extreme."

113. For a full discussion of the importance of trial scenes in Euripides, see Michael Lloyd, *The Agon in Euripides* (Oxford, 1992

For (RE)MAKING TRAGEDY: *pp. 122-126*
114. Charles Mee, "Culture Writes Us" in *Divine Fire*, ed. Caridad Svich (Back Stage Books, 2005): 9.

115. Mee, *Playing God. Seven Fateful Moments When Great Men Met to Change the World* (Simon and Schuster, 1993): 16 and Chapter VI.

Cover Photo Credits:
Front: Epidauros: CreateSpace Stock Photo
Big Love: Ralf Remshardt
Back: Kevin McCarthy

Bibliography

Andreach, Robert. 2003. *Drawing Upon the Past: Artists and Issues in the Theatre.* New York: Peter Lang.

Andreach, Robert. 1996. "Charles L. Mee's Orestes: A Euripidean Tragedy on Contemporary Transvaluation," *Classical and Modern Literature* 16 (3): 191-202.

Austin, Norman. 1994. Helen *of Troy and her Shameless Phantom.* Cornell University Press.

Bacalzo, Dan. 2001. Review of *The Bacchae 2.1* Posted on TheaterMania. com. New York: March 28.

Burnett, Anne Pippin.1971. *Catastrophe Survived . Euripides Plays of Mixed Reversals.* Oxford.

Bryer, Jackson R., Ed. 1995. *The Playwright's Art. Conversations with Contemporary American Dramatists.* Rutgers University Press.

Cote, David. 2007. "Greek in review: Postmodern dramatist Charles Mee slices and dices ancient tragedy for today," *Time Out New York/* Issue 619: Aug 9–15.

Cummings, Scott. 2006. *Remaking American Theater .Charles Mee, Anne Bogart and the SITI Company.* Cambridge.

DiGaetani, John L. 1991. *A Search for a Postmodern Theater. Interviews with Contemporary Playwrights.* Westport, CT: Greenwood.

Dodds, E. R. 1960. *Euripides' Bacchae.* Text and Commentary. Oxford.

Easterling, P.E. 1997. *The Cambridge Companion to Greek Tragedy.* Cambridge.

Easterling, P.E. and Bernard M.W. Knox (eds). 1989. *The Cambridge History of Classical Literature.* Cambridge.

Ehrenreich, Barbara. 2007. *Dancing in the Streets, A History of Collective Joy.* London: Granta Books.

Foley, Helene. 1991. "Modern Performance and Adaptation of Greek Tragedy," Presidential Address/American Philological Association *TAPA* 129: 1-12.

Fuchs, Elinor. 1994. "Play as Landscape: Another Version of Pastoral," *Theater* 25: 44-51.

Green, Amy S. 1994. *The Revisionist Stage. American Directors Reinvent the Classics.* Cambridge.

Hartigan, Karelisa. 1991. *Ambiguity and Self-Deception. The Apollo and Artemis Plays of Euripides.* Frankfurt am Mein: Peter Lang.

Hartigan, Karelisa V. 1995. *Greek Tragedy on the American Stage. Ancient Drama in the Commercial Theater, 1882-1994.* Westport, CT: Greenwood.

Hartigan, Karelisa. 2008. *Performance and Cure. Drama and Healing in Ancient Greece and Contemporary America.* London: Duckworth.

Hitchcock, Laura. 2006. Review of *Agamemnon* for *A CurtainUp Review* (July 7/ Los Angeles), posted on The Internet Theater Magazine of Reviews: www.curtainup.com.

Hitchcock, Laura. 2007. "Charles Mee's Take on Iphigenia," *A CurtainUp Review* (January 14 /Los Angeles) posted in The Internet Theater Magazine of Reviews, www.curtainup.com.

Holland, Peter. 1989. "Space: the final frontier" in H. Scolnicov and P. Holland, *The Play Out of Context: Transferring Plays from Culture to Culture*: 45 – 62.

Johnston, David. 2009. "Building Bridges," Program notes for the production of his translation of *Dog in the Manger* at the American Shakespeare Theatre (February-March).

Knox, Bernard. 1979. *Word and Action: Essays on the Ancient Theater.* Johns Hopkins University Press.

Lloyd Michael.1992. *The Agon in Euripides.* Oxford.

Luschnig, C.A.E.1980. "Men and Gods in Euripides' *Hippolytus*," *Ramus* 9: 89-100.

Mandell, Joseph. 2001. "Falling In, Falling Out: Love's Cycle Of Rebirth," *The New York Times*: Arts (2 September).

Marranca, Bonnie and Gautam Dasbupta. 1999. *Conversations on Art and Performance.* John Hopkins University Press.

McCarter, Jeremy. 2007."Sing, O Mash-up! Charles Mee's *Iphigenia 2.0* seems t to incorporate everything he's ever heard or read—mostly for the better. *The Theatre Review* (September 10).

McDonald, Marianne. 1992. *Ancient Sun, Modern Light.* Columbia University Press.

Mee, Charles. 2004. "Shaped, in bits, drips and quips," in "Playwrights on Writing," *LA Times* (October 24).

Mee, Charles L. 1999. *A Nearly Normal Life.* Boston: Little, Brown & Company.

Mee, Charles L. 1993. *Playing God. Seven Fateful Moments When Great Men Met to Change the World.* New York: Simon & Schuster.

Mee, Charles, the (re)making project at http://www.charlesmee.org/html/about.html.

Mee, Erin B. 2002. "Shattered and Fucked Up and Full of Wreckage: The Words and Works of Charles L. Mee". *TDR: The Drama Review* 46 (3): 83–104.

Meineck, Peter. 1998. trans. *Aeschylus: Oresteia.* Indianapolis, IN: Hackett.

Morris, Steven Leigh. 2006. "Greek Love: Charles L. Mee's *Agamemnon*, and Sarah Ruhl's *Demeter in the City*" in *LA Weekly* (June 22):1.

Oberhelman, Steven.1987. "The Diagnostic Dream in Ancient Medical Theory and Practice," *Bulletin of the History of Medicine* 61-1: 47-60.

Redmond, James. 1989. "If the salt have lost his savour": some 'useful' plays in and out of context on the London Stage" in H. Scolnicov and P. Holland, *The Play Out of Context. Transferring Plays from Culture to Culture.* Cambridge: 63-88.

Rehm, Rush. 2003. *Radial Theatre: Greek Tragedy and the Modern World.* London: Duckworth.

Reilly, Kara. 2005. "A Collage Reality (Re) Made: The Postmodern Dramaturgy of Charles L. Mee". *American Drama* 14 (2): 56–71.

Rohrs, Alison. 2007. Review of *Orestes 2.0,* at the HERE Arts Center, "It\'s All Greek to Mee" on *OffOffonline.com* (March 31).

Roisman, Hanna (1999). *Nothing Is As It Seems.* Lanham, MD: University Press of America.

Saltzman, Simon. 2007. *Iphigeneia 2.0. A CurtainUp Review* (August 22/ New York) posted in The Internet Theater Magazine of Reviews, www. curtainup.com).

Scarry, Elaine. 1985. *The Body in Pain. The Making and Unmaking of the World.* Oxford.

Schanke, Robert Al, editor. 2007. *Angels in the American Theater: Patrons, Patronage, and Philanthropy.* Carbondale, IL: University of Southern Illinois Press.

Schleuter, Jennifer. 2005. "Staging Versailles: Charles L. Mee and the Re-Presentation of History". *The Journal of American Drama and Theatre* 17 (3): 5–77.

Scolnicov, Hanna and Peter Holland.1989. *The Play Out of Context. Transferring Plays from Culture to Culture.* Cambridge.

Segal, Charles. 1986. *Interpreting Greek Tragedy: Myth, Poetry, Text .* Cornell University Press.

Shaked, Gershon. 1989. "The Play: Gateway to Cultural Dialogue," in H. Scolnicov and P. Holland, *The Play Out of Context: Transferring Plays from Culture to Culture*. Cambridge University Press: 7-24.

Shay, Jonathan. !994. Achilles in Vietnam. Combat Trauma and the Undoing of Character. New York: Scribner.

Signature Theatre: "Getting to Know Mee," *Signature Edition (excerpts)*. *http://signaturetheatre.org/0708/iphigenia* 2.htm. Retrieved July 26, 2009.

Sommer, Elyse. 2001. *True Love*. A *CurtainUp* Review (26 November).

Sponberg, Arvid F. 1991. *Broadway Talks. What Professionals Think about Commercial Theater in America*. Westport, CT: Greenwood.

Svich, Caridad. 2005. *Divine Fire. Eight Contemporary Plays Inspired by the Greeks*. New York: Backstage Books.

Zeitlin, Froma. 1990. "Playing the Other: Theater, Theatricality, and the Feminine in Greek Drama" in Froma I. Zeitlin and John Winkler, eds. *Nothing to Do with Dionysos? Athenian Drama in its Social Context*. Princeton: 63-74

Index

Made in the USA
San Bernardino, CA
03 January 2014